UNIVERSITY OF NORTH CAROLINA AT CHAPEL HILL
DEPARTMENT OF ROMANCE LANGUAGES

NORTH CAROLINA STUDIES
IN THE ROMANCE LANGUAGES AND LITERATURES

Founder: URBAN TIGNER HOLMES

Distributed by:

UNIVERSITY OF NORTH CAROLINA PRESS

CHAPEL HILL
North Carolina 27514
U.S.A.

NORTH CAROLINA STUDIES IN THE
ROMANCE LANGUAGES AND LITERATURES
Number 200

TWO AGAINST TIME

TWO AGAINST TIME
A STUDY OF THE VERY PRESENT WORLDS OF PAUL CLAUDEL AND CHARLES PÉGUY

BY

JOY NACHOD HUMES

CHAPEL HILL

NORTH CAROLINA STUDIES IN THE ROMANCE
LANGUAGES AND LITERATURES
U.N.C. DEPARTMENT OF ROMANCE LANGUAGES
1978

Library of Congress Cataloging in Publication Data

Humes, Joy.
  Two against time.

  (North Carolina studies in the Romance languages and literatures; 200)
  Bibliography: p.
  1. Claudel, Paul, 1868-1955 — Criticism and interpretation. 2. Péguy, Charles Pierre, 1873-1914 — Criticism and interpretation. 3. Time in literature. I. Title. II. Series.

PQ2605.L2Z683   840'.9'00912   78-3474
ISBN 0-8076-9200-9

I. S. B. N. 0-8076-9200-9

DEPÓSITO LEGAL: V. 742 - 1978   I.S.B.N. 84-399-8132-5
ARTES GRÁFICAS SOLER, S. A. - JÁVEA, 28 - VALENCIA (8) - 1978

For Charles G. Whiting, teacher and friend,
in appreciation . . .

Time past and time future
What might have been and what has been
Point to one end, which is always present.
                        T. S. ELIOT

TABLE OF CONTENTS

	Page
INTRODUCTION	11
I. GENESIS	29
II. TIME	58
III. ...AND TIME AGAIN	80
IV. THE ONCE & FUTURE WORLD	101
V. RE-PRESENTATION	136
BIBLIOGRAPHY	169

INTRODUCTION

I first became acquainted with the work of Charles Péguy when, as a young student at the Sorbonne on a typical junior-year-abroad, I happened upon a used copy of *Le Mystère des Saints innocents*. I read ... and read ... and am still reading. Only much later did I discover Paul Claudel. I think he interested me mainly because, while he stood in such direct contrast to Péguy — physically, poetically, even religiously — still the two shared so many of the same preoccupations. Both writers, however different, must be regarded as leaders in the religious and intellectual movement which was taking place in France around the turn of the century.

In this introduction I would like only to touch upon some of the points of contrast and comparison, some of the common themes and values which occur in the works (and occupied the lives) of both poets. In succeeding chapters I will try to show that this thematic concordance is not at all accidental, but stems from a rejection of the modern world (for Péguy, *le monde moderne* and *les modernes* are terms of contempt) and all it stands for — materialism, technology, dehumanization, deterioration of moral and esthetic values, loss of faith, and finally, that sickness unto death, Despair. Both poets, I believe, do not merely transcend time: they reject it as it is generally conceived, and more, they re-create it. Each builds in his own work a new time structure by means of which he will inject into the *present* values which seemed to have been lost. Each, in his own way, ultimately is able to formulate a doctrine of Hope. But before attempting any comparisons, it might be well to situate Claudel and Péguy in their time — their historical present.

During the last fifteen-odd years of the nineteenth century and up to the outbreak of World War I, France underwent a veritable spiritual renaissance. Names of the literary (and political) great or near-great who converted to Roman Catholicism come at once to mind: one of the first, Paul Bourget, philosopher and novelist; Ferdinand Brunetière, writer and editor; Pierre Loti, novelist; the socialist, Léon Bloy; Joris-Karl Huysmans, symbolist poet; Francis James and Jacques Rivière, both disciples of Claudel, Jacques and Raïssa Maritain, saved from a suicide pact by Henri Bergson; Joseph Lotte, Péguy's great friend; and of course, Paul Claudel and Charles Péguy themselves.

Much of the credit for this spirit of renewal must be given to that remarkable negotiator, Pope Leo XIII. When Pope Pius IX died in 1878, the papacy was in a sorry state indeed. Pope Pius had alienated intellectuals throughout Europe by his 1870 encyclical, proclaiming papal infallibility. Faced with political difficulties as well, Pius retreated into an isolated spirituality.

The new pope thought of himself as a builder of Christian nations. First, however, he needed to strengthen the Vatican itself. It was menaced by the new Italian republic which Pius had refused to recognize. Catholics were being persecuted in Lutheran Germany. Neither Protestant England — with her own religious troubles in Ireland — nor schismatic Russia was apt to be of help, so Leo turned toward France. Here was a Catholic nation which might be of support and in which the Church certainly stood in need of rebuilding.

Relations between the Church and the French government had been strained since the founding of the Third Republic. In society and in the economy the French clergy still held entrenched, privileged, and much-resented positions. Not only had they grown increasingly out of touch with the poor and the new working class, and callous toward their sufferings, but they were by and large royalists, fomenting or at least supporting unsuccessful attempts to restore the monarchy and refusing to recognize the Republic as legitimate. Because of this, anti-clericalism among government officials, intellectuals, and the working class was strong. Between 1880 and 1882 the National Assembly passed three bills secularizing the schools, and by 1882 the separation between church and state was complete.

Leo moved discreetly but surely. First, he encouraged the so-called Union of Fribourg, under the leadership of the Bishop of Geneva. These were international conferences, held in 1885 and 1891 in Fribourg, Switzerland, expressly to study what was happening in the great Catholic countries in reference to limiting working hours, fostering trade unionism, alleviating unemployment and disease among the poor.

Then, in 1891, having somewhat laid the groundwork for it, Pope Leo issued his encyclical, *de Rerum Novarum*. In it, he warned that Christians could no longer ignore the abuses brought about by capitalism and the philosophy of laissez-faire. The Church, he said, must be concerned. A few months later he again surprised French Catholics, this time by departing from tradition and publishing an encyclical in the French religious press, entitled *Au milieu des sollicitudes* (In Solicitude). In this second encyclical, Leo made it clear that he felt restoration of the monarchy in France was most unlikely. Therefore he urged Catholics to accept the *de facto* republican government, even though it was not legitimate. According to him, although the nature of civil authority in France could not be regarded as being derived from God, still it was permissible — even necessary — for the welfare of society to accept and obey such a government. In effect, he called on French Catholics on the right to rally to the support of the Republic.

Leo also took steps to put the clergy back in touch with the people. Writing to his bishops, the pope called on them to accept and support the government, and to foster greater democratization and activity among the young priests. To the Bishop of Coutances he wrote in 1893, "Advise your priests to give up cloistering themselves within the walls of their churches and presbyteries and to go out to the people, doing all they possibly can for the workers, the poor, the members of the lower class." "At the time, my boy, we felt almost as though the earth were trembling under our feet," says the parish priest of Torcy, speaking of those days, in Bernanos' *Journal d'un curé de campagne*.

The bishops, as might have been expected, were less enthusiastic than Leo would have wished, and despite his prodding, remained a conservative force within the French Church. The young priests, on the contrary, did go to the people, and in fact became so vocal, through liberal Catholic journals such as *La Concorde,* that Leo himself finally had to rein them in.

The term "social catholicism" did not come into general usage in France until 1897, but early in the 1870's two very different groups, sometimes cooperating with one another, were seeking social reform through religious institutions. On the one side were rightist, even monarchist Catholics of the nobility, who took a paternalistic attitude toward the people and placed their faith for reform in authority and established institutions; on the other, workers joined by intellectuals, who hoped to gain more power for the people through democratization. Three such individuals deserve mention because of the scope of their joint efforts: the Comte de la Tour du Pin, an aristocrat who never accepted the Republic, Albert de Mun, an army officer who finally but reluctantly did, and Léon Harmel, a deeply religious factory owner. La Tour du Pin and Albert de Mun dreamt of an alliance between the aristocracy and the people, of groups of workers centered around chapels, being instructed in religious, economic, social matters by their priests and their noble benefactors. In 1871, with this ideal in mind, the *Œuvre des Cercles* was founded.

Léon Harmel, the third mentioned, may properly be described as a practical visionary. In 1854, when he was only twenty-five, his father's health obliged the son to take over management of the family spinning factory, near Rheims. His father had already set up some social organization among his employees. Harmel elaborated on this until he had built a system that touched all aspects of the workers' lives. There were boarding houses, an emergency fund, work councils, a committee to improve technical processes, insurance plans, even arrangements to insure young girls of doweries. Most importantly, all of this was run democratically, by the workers themselves. Harmel's formula, "The good of the worker by the worker and with the worker. Never without him, and especially, never against him."[1] When Harmel was asked to help organize the

---

[1] Adrien Dansette, *Religious History of Modern France,* II, tr. John Dingle (N.Y.: Herder & Herder, 1961), p. 121.

In the case of Claudel and Péguy I have made extensive use of the Pléiade editions (v. Bibliography) of their work. For Claudel I have used the Pléiade's *Œuvre poétique, Théâtre* I, II, and his *Journal;* for Péguy, *Œuvre poétique, Œuvres en prose* (1898-1908) and *Œuvres en prose.* All page numbers, unless otherwise indicated, refer to these editions. It has also been necessary, how-

Œuvre des Cercles, he gladly acceded, and spent six years travelling around France, founding study groups and in general trying to get the movement off the ground. Ultimately the fact that La Tour du Pin saw the circles as being run by noblemen, and Harmel, as being democratically organized and fostering leadership among the workers, led to dissension and final abandonment of the effort.

A new intellectual climate which would favor a spiritual revival was also beginning to develop. Scientism, child of Comte's positivism, and its literary counterpart, naturalism, had dominated French thinking in the last third of the nineteenth century. Now both seemed to have run their course. Renan and Taine would soon be dead, Renan in 1892, Taine a year later. Zola, dean of naturalism, was still writing, but he would die in 1902, his disciple, Huysmans, would evolve from naturalism to symbolism, from disbelief to religious mysticism. As early as 1875 the academician Emile Boutroux had published *la Contingence des lois de la nature,* in which he stated that since every science had laws of its own, total determinism was not possible. Ferdinand Brunetière used his *Revue des deux mondes* to launch scathing attacks first on naturalism, then on scientism (which he tended to confound with science itself), and William James, in *The Varieties of Religious Experience* (1902) suggested there might be pragmatic bases for religious faith. In short, intellectual leaders were seriously questioning the doctrine that all phenomena could be explained and problems solved in scientific terms of cause and effect.

Among the anti-determinists, the philosopher Henri Bergson was by far the most influential. In *Matière et Mémoire* (1896) he sought to show the reality of the soul. In his *Essai sur les données immédiates de la conscience* he claimed that scientific truths could only be fragmentary, and that absolute truths were attainable through intuition. He particularly stressed human freedom. In *l'Evolution créatrice* (1907) he argued that we live in a God-created universe. His effect upon the Maritains and Péguy would be hard to overestimate, and in the latter's case, will be examined in depth.

---

ever, to refer to the Gallimard editions of both authors. When such references are initially made, they are so indicated. Later references merely give the book title. I have also frequently cited material found in the invaluable *Feuillets de l'Amitié Charles Péguy,* edited by Auguste Martin, and hereafter referred to simply as *Feuillets.*

Finally, there was the Dreyfus case, exploding on France in 1894, dividing the people into two opposing camps of Dreyfusards and anti-Dreyfusards. The country had been well-prepared. In 1886 Eduard Drumont had had spectacular success with his two-volume *La France Juive,* in which he had viciously attacked Jews and their supposed deleterious effect upon society. This book was followed by others, equally scurrilous, and in 1892 Drumont founded *La Libre Parole,* an anti-Semitic daily which drew most of its subscribers from the Catholic middle class and the older members of the lower clergy. When the cry went up that a Jew had betrayed France a great many people were ready to believe, no questions asked. In the beginning political, as more and more evidence turned up to cast doubt on Dreyfus' guilt, the affair took on moral and even religious tones. Should an innocent man be left in prison to spare France and her military leaders disgrace? Some very high-ranking persons thought so. The attitude of the French clergy does them little credit: by and large they greeted the affair with silence and hoped it would go away. The pope, however, saw the affair — as did Péguy — on a mystical plane, and went so far as to compare the martyrdom of Dreyfus with that of Christ. In an interview with a *Figaro* reporter in March, 1899, Leo said, "Our religion has already hallowed the memory of many thousands of martyrs. The lesson we must learn is from our master on Calvary. Happy is the victim whom God recognizes as sufficiently just to confound his cause with that of his own Son who was sacrificed."

Adrien Dansette, in his two-volume *Religious History of Modern France,* has sought to explain how what was essentially a political affair could become the focus of such religious intensity in the case of someone like Péguy:

> As we have already indicated several times in different ways, Péguy's distinction between the mystical outlook and politics is of capital importance in the history of the Church. The Dreyfus affair illustrates this most clearly. If we look at Christianity's message of love in the light of the life of Christ, who was the victim of the greatest judicial error in history, and in the light cast by the gospel narrative, it can hardly be denied that the Christian mystery is essentially Dreyfusard. Péguy, who was still far away from the precints of the temple in which his soul had its habitation, and into which his body was never to penetrate, seemed

by his aspirations toward truth and justice to be more Catholic than most Catholics.[2]

At the beginning of the 20th century social Catholicism, or to use Pope Leo's term, Christian democracy, had received surface setbacks. The democratic priests had been too enthusiastic and had alienated land and factory owners. In 1901 Leo felt obliged to issue his encyclical, *Graves de Communi,* recalling to the priests the necessity of cooperation between the working classes and established authorities. The *Œuvre des Cercles* had collapsed. Despite papal urging, the higher clergy in France remained aloof, conservative. Yet the seed had been sown which would bring about a powerful *ralliement* both to the Church and to the Republic. Young, conservative Catholics had been encouraged to accept and even support the Republic, and to involve themselves in the struggles of the people. Workers and intellectuals outside the Church had been gladdened to see the Church begin to take an active interest in their own idealistic goals. From opposite poles the two groups were moving toward one another. This was the backdrop against which Claudel and Péguy walked onto stage to play out their respective roles, Claudel from the monarchist right wing, Péguy from the socialist left.

Both converts to Roman Catholicism (Péguy, in spirit, at least) and sharing common themes and concerns, yet how different in temperament, style and approach are Claudel and Péguy! The contrast extends to and is in part explained by the disparity of their lives.

Claudel's choice of diplomatic career took him to the far corners of the earth. Although he returned quite frequently to France and carried on a lively correspondence with friends there, he remained the perpetual exile, surrounded by peoples and cultures not his own. Some of the isolation he must often have felt finds expression in *l'Esprit et l'Eau,* which I will examine later, and may explain the sort of interior expansion found in that and other poems.

Péguy, on the other hand, traveled practically not at all. A student trip to Orange was the longest voyage he ever made. He passed his days in the tiny office at 8 rue de la Sorbonne, writing,

---

[2] Ibid., p. 176.

editing, and despite his weakened eyes, proofreading his *Cahiers de la Quinzaine*. In contrast to Claudel, the exile, Péguy referred to himself as *enraciné* in French soil.

His *Cahiers* were perpetually on the brink of financial disaster, even though the subscriber list boasted some of the most eminent literary and political names of the time. His poetic publications caused hardly a ripple in critical circles, a fact which deeply discouraged him.

Claudel, on the contrary, was an eminent success in his double career of diplomat and author. Even the ironic André Gide felt intimidated in his presence. After one of his last visits with Claudel Gide confided to his *Journal,* "Devant Claudel je n'ai sentiment que de mes manques; il me domine; il me surplombe; il a plus de base et de surface, plus de santé, d'argent, de génie, de puissance, d'enfants, de foi, etc. . . . que moi. Je ne songe qu'à filer doux." [3] From Gide's descriptions of Claudel one gets the impression of a man of enormous vitality and self-confidence, fully aware of his power and success. "Jeune, il avait l'air d'un clou; il a l'air maintenant d'un marteau-pilon. Front très haut, mais assez large; visage sans nuances, comme taillé au couteau; cou de taureau continué tout droit par la tête, où l'on sent que la passion monte congestionner aussitôt le cerveau." In the same passage he compared Claudel to "un cyclone figé." [4]

Although Péguy, according to his biographers, had a certain "présence," he was not physically prepossessing. He was small, spoke in a monotonous and rather unpleasant voice, dressed carelessly, and even though relatively young, was prematurely worn out by the labor involved in preparing the *Cahiers*. He reminded his friend, Madame Simone (Pauline Benda) of a village schoolmaster.

These contrasts in temperament and life style seem at times reflected in their respective forms of poetic expression. Where Claudel creates a language which fairly explodes with power, Péguy most often walks humbly, speaking of simple things in simple words. Claudel's symbolism tends to be subtle, sometimes cerebral; Péguy's symbols are more obvious, often drawn from agriculture, and intelligible to the peasant-farmer. The difference between the two poets

---

[3] André Gide, *Journal* (Paris: Gallimard, 1949), p. 22.
[4] Ibid.

is similar to that between the artist and the artisan: Claudel consciously asumes the role of the artist-priest in the service of God; Péguy, commenting on his own *Tapisseries* (de Ste. Geneviève, de Notre Dame) likens himself to the medieval craftsman, weaving his design, thread by thread.

Péguy drew his own comparison between Claudel which I find quite accurate and penetrating. He explained to Ernest Psichari and Henri Massis:

> Claudel manque de simplicité, Il recherche l'extrême, le périlleux, l'exceptionnel... Il lui faut toujours franchir des abîmes sur la corde raide... Son christianisme a quelque chose de provoquant! Entendez-moi bien, car je ne veux pas, il ne doit pas y avoir, il ne peut pas y avoir de malentendus entre Claudel et moi. L'un et l'autre nous travaillons, nous œuvrons dans le sacré... Mais, moi, je ne suis pas l'homme des cimes, je suis l'homme de la plaine... Je marche avec la piétalle, moi, je prends le chemin de tout le monde, je reste avec tout le monde...[5]

Perhaps because their life styles were so dissimilar, the two never met, although they shared mutual literary acquaintances, André Gide and the Maritains among them (v. Raïssa Maritain's *Les Grandes Amitiés* — translated as *We Were Friends Together*). Gide was the first to link the names of the two poets. In an enthusiastic review of *Le Mystère de la Charité de Jeanne d'Arc* in March 1910 in the Nouvelle Revue Française he wrote: "Je l'entr'ouvre et presque aussitôt je n'ai plus d'attention pour rien d'autre. L'étonnant livre! Rien, depuis *l'Arbre* de Claudel, ne m'avait imposé davantage."[6]

It was Gide, also, who brought about the first indirect contact between them. *Jeanne* had appeared in January of 1910. In February Gide sent a copy to Claudel, with a note explaining, "Vous recevrez aussi le *Jeanne d'Arc* de Péguy — que je vous offre parce qu'il *n'osait pas* vous l'envoyer et parce que je trouve ce livre admirable."[7]

---

[5] Henri Massis, *Notre Ami Psichari* (Paris: Flammarion, 1936), p. 140.

[6] Gide, "Journal sans dates," NRF, III, 1 (March 1910), pp. 383-400.

[7] *Correspondance: Paul Claudel-André Gide* (1899-1926). Ed. Robert Mallet (Paris: Gallimard, 1949), p. 119.

Claudel, who had imagined Péguy as "le type de dreyfusard, de l'anarchiste, de l'intellectuel, du tolstoïsant et autres horreurs" was amazed that a book of such spiritual beauty could have been written by this man. "Mais voici un livre au contraire du plus délicat sentiment chrétien et catholique, les pages sur la Passion sont de la plus profonde et de la plus émouvante beauté, et de tous côtés on trouve de ces choses que seules peut savoir un cœur profondément religieux." Because of his opinion of Péguy, Claudel felt sure that all this was only "literature" and lamented: "Un livre si *édifiant* écrit par un destructeur!" Predictably, given his very conservative Catholicism, he critisized Péguy's characterization of Jeanne. "J'aime mieux madame Gervaise que Jeannette dont il a fait une sorte de protestante têtue, ne sachant que faire des reproches au bon Dieu."[8] In Gide's reply he assured Claudel Péguy's religious convictions were genuine, calling him "Péguy-Paul de Tarse" and asking permission to send Claudel's letter to Péguy... "que je sais plus soucieux de votre opinion que de toute autre."[9] *

In a later letter Claudel asked Gide to send him other works by Péguy, adding, "J'aimerais à me former une idée plus nette de cet écrivain abondant... Je le vois un peu comme l'apprenti sorcier de Goethe avec des papiers débordant de tous côtés de sa table de travail, ruisselant par les fenêtres, giglant [sic] par les soupiraux."[10] Gide relayed this request to Péguy, who, delighted, sent Claudel *Notre Jeunesse* with the inscription:

> exemplaire
> pour monsieur Paul Claudel
> samedi 6 août 1910
> voici, monsieur, une chronique
> des durs temps présents
> je suis votre dévoué
> Charles Péguy [11]

---

[8] Cited by Henri de Lubac & Jean Bastaire, *Claudel et Péguy* (Paris: Aubier-Montaigne, 1974), p. 47.

[9] *Correspondance*, p. 124.

* Gide did send the letter on to Péguy. It was acquired by the Centre Péguy in Orléans in 1968, which is why it doesn't appear in *Correspondence: Claudel-Gide.*

[10] Ibid., p. 142.

[11] *Feuillets*, no. 85, June 1961, p. 29.

Far from helping Claudel to form a clearer idea of Péguy, *Notre Jeunesse* further perplexed the former. He read it at once, and four days later dispatched a long letter to the author in which he expresses both his admiration and consternation. "Toute cette partie du livre si belle, si éloquente, où vous parlez des Juifs et de Bernard Lazare a arraché de force mon admiration, bien que je sois fort peu sympathique aux thèses et aux gens que vous soutenez." An ardent anti-Dreyfusard himself he cannot comprehend Péguy's passionate defense of Dreyfus, nor how he can feel the affair is intimately linked with the Christian mission. "Quel dommage de trouver un vrai Français, un soldat de Saint Louis (je pense à vos admirable pages sur le péché mortel) combattant avec des gens tout primitifs et imbus de la malédiction de Dieu." At one point in his letter Claudel becomes so incensed that he calls the Jews, "ces punaises à face humaine." One can imagine Péguy's reaction, since many of his closest friends — and the woman he loved — were Jewish! Claudel ends his letter with a plea for Péguy to clarify his position:

> Je vous demande pardon de m'être ainsi échauffé, mais vos livres me donnent une haute opinion de vous, je vous aime beaucoup, et je voudrais mieux savoir votre position actuelle. Car si vous êtes chrétien, vous êtes ami de l'ordre; si vous aimez l'ordre, vous reconnaissez l'autorité: et quelle autorité y a-t-il, si vous le jugez comme ayant vous-même autorité sur elle.[12]

(In all fairness to Claudel it should be noted that his position toward the Jews softened in later years, and in his interviews with Jean Amrouche which form *Mémoires improvisés* he admitted that he had not been on the right side of the Dreyfus affair). Péguy did not even answer the letter, nor did he send Claudel copies of his next two works, *Victor-Marie comte Hugo* (Oct. 1910) and *Œuvres choisies* (April 1911). Perhaps conscious of the deep affront he had given Péguy, Claudel graciously asked that his name be withdrawn from consideration for the Grand Pris de Littérature de l'Académie française in June 1911, as it would have put him in contention with Péguy. Péguy seemed unaware of the gesture at the time. It was

---

[12] Letter from Claudel to Péguy, August 10, 1910, *Feuillets*, no. 165, January 1971, pp. 28-31.

only when Claudel wrote to Joseph Lotte, who had founded the *Bulletin des professeurs catholiques de l'université* in January 1911, praising the "communiqué" which Péguy had written anonymously for the July issue that the latter resumed correspondence, sending Claudel *Un nouveau théologien M. Laudet*.[13] Claudel's unequivocal admiration encouraged Péguy to send him *Le Porche du mystère de la deuxième vertu*, inscribed "au poète des Hymnes et des Grandes Odes, cet avancement de la deuxième théogale, Charles Péguy."[14] In December of 1911, knowing that Claudel intended to return to Paris for Christmas, Péguy wrote to him, requesting (almost demanding) a meeting:

> Monsieur,
>
> Vous êtes sans doute rentré. Je veux vous remercier de tout ce que vous avez fait pour moi à l'Académie. Je veux, si vous voulez, causer plus avant. Je veux d'autant plus vous voir que je considère comme un événement de ma vie d'avoir enfin établi une communication directe avec Paul Claudel. Qu'il fût un grand poète, je le savais de longue date; mais qu'il fût aussi un grand cœur, c'est ce que j'ai découvert avec une grande joie dans le courant de cet été.
>
> Je suis, Monsieur, votre très respectueusement dévoué,
> Charles Péguy [15]

Claudel did not respond to the invitation. He, in turn, may have been offended as Henri de Lubac and Jean Bastaire suggest in *Claudel et Péguy* by the almost cornelian tone of the letter, the three *je veux*'s and the brevity of it. The authors of that book observe, "A défaut du 'à moi, comte, deux mots' de Rodrigue à Gormas, on retrouve le climat de haute émulation qui règne entre Horace et Curiace, Polyeucte et Sévère."[16] Péguy clearly considered himself Claudel's equal and addressed him as such. Whatever the reason, the meeting never took place, and what an interesting — and stormy — one it might have been.

---

[13] Lubac & Bastaire, pp. 140-143.
[14] *Feuillets*, no. 85, June 1961, p. 30.
[15] Letter from Péguy to Claudel, December 15, 1911, *Feuillets*, no. 165, January 1971, p. 32.
[16] Lubac & Bastaire, p. 149.

In spite of what must have seemed a slight, Péguy sent Claudel a copy of *Le Mystère des Saints innocents* in April 1912. The latter's response this time was prompt and very warm: "Merci, Monsieur, pour votre nouveau volume de *Jeanne d'Arc,* digne des deux qui l'ont précédé. Toute la chevalerie française n'a pas péri sur les champs de Poitiers et d'Azincourt. Vous nous rendez la vieille Chanson de Geste, pleine de son vieil entrain populaire, de Roland et de Brut." [17]

Claudel's opinion of his work meant a great deal to Péguy, for he greatly admired the "poètes des Hymnes et des Grandes Odes" — as a *poet.* Claudel, the dramatist, however, was quite another matter. According to Jules Riby, "il avait *l'Otage* en horreur" [18] (an opinion which this writer shares). As for *l'Annonce faite à Marie,* he told Madame Favre and Psichari:

> C'est regressif. Et quelle impiété dans ce miracle inventé de l'enfant — le seul qu'il ne fallait pas inventer puisqu'on est sûr avec cela de faire pleurer la salle. Trop facile. D'une façon générale, le catholicisme de Claudel manque de charité. Claudel est un grand artiste, mais il n'est pas intelligent. [19]

Despite the praise Claudel had bestowed on Péguy during the latter's lifetime, and despite a certain remote kinship he apparently felt for him, he was never able to resolve to his satisfaction his doubts about Péguy either as an artist or as a Catholic. These two "vocations" were so inextricably linked in Claudel's mind (v. *Art poétique*) that he could separate them only with great difficulty, and the suspect, uncertain aspect of Péguy's conversion may have affected Claudel's later assessment of his art. In 1930, for instance, he wrote to his friend, Guiberteau, "J'honore Péguy, mais froidement. Nous marchons dans des chemins bien séparés et qui ne se rencontrent qu'en un point idéal. Il est Français avant tout et moi je suis catholique avant tout." [20]

---

[17] Letter from Claudel to Péguy, May 23, 1912, *Feuillets,* no. 165, Jan. 1971, p. 33.
[18] Letter from Jules Riby to Joseph Lotte, Oct. 11, 1911, *Feuillets,* no. 102, August 1963, p. 8.
[19] Journal of Ernest Psichari, *Feuillets,* no. 112, Feb. 1965, p. 24.
[20] Letter to Philippe Guiberteau from Claudel, Apr. 12, 1930, *Feuillets,* no. 114, June 1965, p. 30.

When, in January 1939, he was called upon to speak at the dedication ceremonies of the former headquarters of *Les Cahiers de la quinzaine,* 8, rue de la Sorbonne, he made no allusion to Péguy's poetic works, speaking only of the influence of the *Cahiers* and Péguy's personal heroic example.[21]

He was even harsher in a letter to Mme. Romain Rolland in 1945:

> Je salue Péguy, mais je ne peux pas dire que je ressens pour lui une sympathie profonde. Nos natures restent étrangères. Je ne trouve pas non plus que ce soit un grand écrivain . . . je plains cette pauvre âme qui n'a cessé de tourner autour de l'autel, sans réussir à obtenir la communion.[22]

In summary, then, relations between these two great French Catholic poets were always indirect, lasted only a few years, and were often quite cool. There are really no provable cross influences. Yet, despite these contrasts in their lives and works, there are many points of comparison, which I should like to explore.

Both men rejected the modern world as it was, yet neither retreated from it, working instead to change and better it. True, Claudel had considered entering the Benedictine order, but when he received what he felt was a clear "rejection" he pursued a distinguished carrer and placed his pen at God's service. His *Contacts et Circonstances,* for example, attest to the wide range of his political and social concerns. Péguy devoted his life energies to the realization of his socialistic vision and strove, against high odds, to keep French socialism honest through the critical weapon of the *Cahiers.* Thus, though both confidently looked forward to an eternal life, they were very much involved in improving this life. There is no contradiction here, for as Péguy observed, "Quand l'éternel livre une bataille au temporel, il faut bien que ce soit une bataille temporelle. Quand le spirituel livre une bataille au matériel, il faut bien que ce soit une bataille matérielle."[23]

---

[21] *Œuvres complètes de Paul Claudel* XVI (Paris: Gallimard, 1950-67), *Contacts et Circumstances.*

[22] Cited by Lubac & Bastaire, p. 177. The letter is in the archives of the Fonds Romain Rolland, Paris.

[23] Charles Péguy, *Œuvres en prose,* Pléiade, II (Paris: Gallimard, 1961), "Note conjointe sur M. Descartes et la philosophie cartésienne," p. 1535.

Both men showed a marked predilection for the Middle Ages, or, more accurately in Péguy's case, for what he termed *ancienne France*. Some of Claudel's work — the *Bestiaire, Les Feuilles des Saints* — was drawn from and inspired by medieval sources and forms. *L'Œil écoute* testifies to his love of Gothic architecture, the *Ode Jubilaire*, to his admiration of Dante. As for Péguy, *ancienne France* is so woven into his entire poetic output as to be inextricable from it.

They shared the same heroes — the great soldier-saints of the Middle Ages. On a questionnaire, in response to "Mes héros dans la vie réelle?" Claudel wrote, "Saint Louis." Jeanne d'Arc heads the list of "mes héroïnes dans l'histoire."[24] When *l'Annonce faite à Marie* at length found its natural home in the fifteenth century it allowed for the introduction of Jeanne's invisible presence. He also devoted to her the beautiful *Jeanne d'Arc au Bûcher*, written in collaboration with Arthur Honneger. Jeanne dominates the work of Péguy, followed by Ste. Geneviève and St. Louis.

Yet, while the same saints and heroes appear in both writers' works, the difference in treatment is remarkable, for where Claudel deals with the "essence" of the saint, Péguy is interested in the human being. Suffering is another common theme, though less emphasized in Péguy. For Claudel it was a means of redemption and purification; for Péguy, an inevitable part of man's existence. Nowhere in Péguy do we find the fascination for pageantry and liturgical rite which characterizes Claudel's work and is, indeed, one aspect of his expansiveness. Péguy is instead drawn to the essentials of Christ's teaching, as distinguished from the dogma and liturgy subsequently developed within the Church.

Perhaps most striking is the role assigned by each to woman. She plays a vital and complex part in Claudel's theater and poetry, a symbol of a collection of symbols, drawn from lay as well as religious sources. Woman is just as central to Péguy's work: Jeanne dominates the mysteries; sainte Geneviève, her *Tapisserie*; Eve, mother of us all, is the subject of a poem by that title. The Virgin is all-pervasive, a sort of life force in the poetry and for the poet himself. Yet sexual love, an important theme in Claudel, is vir-

---

[24] Louis Chaigne, *Vie de Paul Claudel* (Tours: Maison Mame, 1961), p. 9.

tually absent in Péguy's writings which, by his own claim, were "without sin."

Neither poet is concerned with historical accuracy (the one exception, Péguy's early *Jeanne d'Arc*) nor tries to re-create an historical period. When Claudel transposed *l'Annonce* to the fifteenth century he took care to provide a backdrop of local color, but indicated himself this was not too important. In the stage directions he wrote: "Tout le drame se passe à la fin d'un Moyen-Age de convention, tel que les poètes du Moyen-Age pouvaient se figurer l'antiquité." This is not to say that the change was a minor one. What Claudel was doing was evoking a particular era as an *imaginative* past which would have certain common associations for most people and against which his drama could unfold. This disregard for the historical time and place is likewise evident in his comment on the setting of his play, *Le Soulier de Satin*: "La scène de ce drame est le monde et plus spécialement l'Espagne à la fin du XVIe siècle. L'auteur s'est permis de comprimer les pays et les époques, de même qu'à la distance voulue plusieurs lignes de montagnes séparées ne sont qu'un seul horizon."

Péguy's notion of *ancienne France* is an extremely complex one and will be studied at length. Here it is enough to say that it is not an historical and geographical time and place, but more nearly an atmosphere, a state of mind. For him, Ste. Geneviève of the fifth century, St. Louis of the thirteenth and Jeanne d'Arc of the fifteenth are all inhabitants of *ancienne France,* and what is more, all contemporaries of one another. Because it is timeless, *ancienne France* is also *present*. Gide understood this paradoxical logic. In his review of *Le Mystère de la Charité* he wrote:

> *Représenter* c'est bien le mot; ici Péguy n'explique rien: il re-présente; c'est à dire, il remet au présent ce passé. Nul archaïsme. Sinon que la misère était plus grande alors, cet alors pourrait être aujourd'hui. Aujourd'hui cette détresse, cette angoisse; aujourd'hui cette sainteté; elle apparaît ici du même coup possible et nécessaire; elle éclot naturellement. Elle ne paraissait pas, alors, plus possible et plus vraisemblable; elle n'est pas moins possible ni moins vraisemblable aujourd'hui.[25]

---

[25] Gide, "Journal sans dates," NRF, III, 1 (March 1910), p. 402.

To re-create — to re-present: this was the self-imposed task and the accomplishment of Paul Claudel and Charles Péguy. In Chapter I, "Genesis," I will deal with the events and the formative influences in their early lives, the themes, problems, struggles nascent in their first works. Chapters II and III, "Time," and "... And Time again," will be devoted to an examination of the time structures each poet created in and through his work. In Chapters IV and V, "The Once and Future World," and "Re-presentation," I will try to show the probable reasons each turned toward the past — to the Middle Ages, to *ancienne France*. For I feel they found there a sympathetic environment for many of the values they wished to reintroduce, re-inject as it were, into the modern world: among these, the value of suffering, of womanhood, of the communion of the saints, of innocence. In their imaginative evocations of the past both found renewal for the present ... and with it, Hope. This rediscovery if what gives to the work of each poet its vitality, its germinal quality. For, of the three Virtues — Faith, Hope, Charity — if Charity is the greatest, surely Hope in today's world is the most difficult to practice.

CHAPTER I

GENESIS

I

> Car une vie d'homme, comme celle d'une nation,
> a sa période légendaire.
>
> *Contacts et Circonstances*

For Paul Claudel the determining event of his life occurred on Christmas, 1886, at the Vespers service in Notre Dame de Paris. The date marked a personal Easter, his spiritual rebirth.

To understand the great task of creation and re-creation which the mature man was to undertake, it is important to understand what led up to this momentous illumination, and the long spiritual struggle which ensued before his conversion was truly complete. The germ, the *cellule* (a word which recurs often in his work) of creativity was formed and nourished in his childhood and adolescence.

Claudel was born in 1868 in the little town of Villeneuve-sur-Fère, in what is known as the Tardenois region, forming part of the department of Aisne. The town itself, as he liked to point out, is situated at the crossroads of the Reims-Soissons route, a road down which Jeanne d'Arc must have passed on her way to the coronation of the king whom she had saved. Although the family moved away when Claudel was only two years old, it was to Villeneuve, the residence of his maternal grandparents, that he most frequently returned during vacations.

It is clear that these early years at Villeneuve had an enormous influence on both his life and his works; many of the place names that appear in his plays — *Combernon, Geyn,* or those of his characters, *Violaine, Cœuvre,* were taken from neighboring farms or villages. In fact, from his description, Villeneuve would make the perfect setting for the medieval *Méditation on Death.*

> Ceux qui ne connaissent pas la tristesse et ne soupçonnent pas le mèlange d'amertume, de componction et de satisfaction intime, j'allais dire de saturation, avec lequel un chrétien attend le jour du Jugement dernier, n'ont qu'à se rendre à Villeneuve la nuit du Jour des Morts, quand une cloche inlassablement sonne le glas au milieu des torrents d'une pluie glacée.[1]

At the age of eighty-two, reminiscing about his birthplace, he declared, "Il n'y a rien de plus sévère, de plus amer, de plus religieux aussi . . . que ce village de Villeneuve."[2]

Often during the torrential rains he would spend hours "devouring" Butler's *Lives of the Saints,* a book which he said interested him far more than any of the French classics. He speaks lovingly of the local legends, those *histoires du vieux temps,* told him by an old woman servant, Victoire Brunet. One such tale, perhaps recounted by her, was the starting point of *La Jeune Fille Violaine,* later to become his *l'Annonce faite à Marie.* Stories of pilgrimmages to Liesse which, to the young boy were comparable to Marco Polo's voyage to the East, would later inspire Anne Vercor's journey to Jerusalem.[3] On nice days he loved to walk, and walking, composed whole *chansons de geste* in his head. In *Connaissance de l'Est* he tells how he would climb the apple tree in the Villeneuve garden, and how, from the highest branch like a "god on his stem" he would study the conformation of the earth.

Just how reliable these after-the-fact accounts are is questionable. The child, Paul Claudel, as seen by the man, diplomat, poet, is a little like the child-man narrator of *A la Recherche du Temps perdu*

---

[1] *Œuvres complètes de Paul Claudel,* XVI (Paris: Gallimard, 1950-67), *Contacts et Circonstances,* p. 201.

[2] *Mémoires improvisés,* Recueillis par Jean Amrouche. (Paris: Gallimard, 1954), page 12.

[3] For these and other details see *Contacts et Circonstances,* "Mon Pays," XVI.

who benefits, in his re-created state, from all the experience and hindsight of the adult. Claudel would have us believe that in the apple tree he first vowed to circle the earth, to encompass it — "boucler le boucle"[4] — as he did, in fact, in his career and through his poetry. But he is not above (perhaps in all sincerity) fitting the facts to the legend. For instance, in a letter to Gabriel Frizeau he claims to have been born "un dimanche, par un grand soleil, au moment ou sonnaient les cloches de la grand'messe"[5] but official records put his birth hour at 4:00 a.m. In *Mémoires improvisés* he puts the date of *l'Endormie* at 1883,[6] when he would have been fifteen. Whether he was so precocious is really beside the point. What does matter is that his early years at Villeneuve, at Bar-le-Duc, and at his father's home, La Bresse, left a lasting imprint and specifically developed in him a deep kinship with nature.

He liked to think of himself as *enraciné*, close to French village — and peasant — life, and certainly convinced many of his biographers and critics. Louis Gillet, in his lecture series on Claudel, reported the following conversation:

> Aujourd'hui, par ces temps de propagande et de radio, on ne sait plus ce qu'était encore il y a soixante ans la vie dans un village de France: tout le monde se connaissant, on savait tout les uns des autres, les histoires de chaque famille, les mariages, les enfants, les accidents, les maladies, ce qui était arrivé aux garçons et aux filles, aux pères et aux grands-pères. Les murs, les dalles du cimetière parlaient. C'était le livre, la chronique, l'histoire du monde dans un hameau, qui se racontait dans la cuisine, sous le manteau de la cheminée, ou l'été, devant le porche, sous le grand orme plein de fables, pareil à un patriarche, entouré d'un banc de pierre circulaire. C'était Saint-Simon au village.[7]

Then Gillet added: "Je découvrais dans le grand poète ce qui est le fond de sa nature, le terrien, le solide et compact paysan qu'il est."[8]

---

[4] Louis Chaigne, *Vie de Paul Claudel* (Tours: Maison Mame, 1961), p. 26.
[5] *Correspondance* 1897-1938, Paul Claudel, Francis Jammes, Gabriel Frizeau avec des lettres de Jacques Rivière. Ed. A. Blanchet (Paris: Gallimard, 1952), p. 51.
[6] Ibid., p. 25.
[7] Louis Gillet, *Claudel, Péguy* (Paris: Ed. du Sagittaire, 1949), p. 34.
[8] Ibid.

However close to nature Claudel may have been, it is a blatant error to imagine him coming from peasant stock. His maternal grandfather, Athanese Cerveaux, was a doctor; his father, a government employee. Of the surviving children (a brother, born in 1863, died at age two weeks) Claudel's two sisters were extremely talented, Louise in music, Camille in sculpture.* When the senior Claudel was assigned to Bar-le-Duc, the boy entered the lycée there directed by the Sœurs de la doctrine chrétienne. When, a year later, his father was transferred to the tiny village of Nogent-sur-Seine, a private tutor was hired for his son. True, Claudel had intimate contact with the peasant class, but he was not of it. Could any farmer, familiar with the back-breaking labor involved, speak of the earth and its fruits as does Anne Vercors? In *Paul Claudel par lui-même*, André Lesort, more accurate and less romantic than Gillet, observes: "Paul Claudel est lié au monde paysan, mais comme les juristes de l'ancienne France l'étaient à la noblesse: ils appartenaient à la noblesse de robe, il appartient à la paysannerie de papier." [9]

One of the events of Claudel's early life which increased a natural tendency toward introspection and actual despondency was the death of his maternal grandfather in 1881. The boy had been very fond of his grandparent, and was taken by his mother to attend the old man in Villeneuve in his last struggle with cancer. To a child of thirteen, the long and painful death watch was a terrible experience, and he afterwards felt that his parents should have spared him of it. He compared the effect it had on his outlook to that of reading Zola's *La Joie de Vivre*. (In *Mémoires improvisés* Claudel puts both events at the same time, but Zola's novel did not actually appear until 1883, two years later).

When Claudel moved to Paris in 1882 with his mother and sisters (so that Camille could study art) his depression was intensified. Only fourteen, he entered the lycée Louis-le-Grand. Already Camille had introduced him to Renan's *Vie de Jésus*; now his entire education was dominated by the influence of Taine and Renan.

---

* Camille Claudel was to become the mistress of the sculptor, Auguste Rodin. His robust genius proved too much for her nervous and sensitive nature, and a few years later she went insane, spending the remainder of a long life in an asylum. In her madness she destroyed the greater part of her work.

[9] Paul-André Lesort, *Paul Claudel par lui-même* (Paris: Ed. du Seuil, 1963), p. 15.

Claudel marks this year as the one in which he lost faith. Christianity became for him no more than a pretty legend, its founder only a good man. History, art, in fact almost everything could be explained in terms of Taine's *race, milieu, moment*. To make matters worse, the boy who had been accustomed to standing first in class failed in his examination for the baccalaureate in 1883.

How bitterly he looked back on this period, and how much he blamed the scepticism of Renan and the determinism of Taine is plain from his virulent attack on both men in the *Magnificat*. Coupling their names with those of Voltaire and Hugo, he writes: "Leur âme est avec les chiens morts, leurs livres sont joints au fumier. / Ils sont morts, et leur nom même après leur mort est un poison et une pourriture." [10]

In 1885, when he had finally succeeded in passing his baccalaureate, his mood was no better. Later, speaking of those days in Paris, he said, "J'ai été le captif de cette Tyr et de cette Babylone, j'ai erré au plus profond de ces entrailles ténébreuses m'attendant à lire sur les plaques indicatrices, plûtot que rue Saint-Jacques et rue du Faubourg-Poissonnière, rue de l'Enfer et carrefour du Désespoir." [11]

He was drawn to Baudelaire, who remained for him his life long the greatest of French poets (he was convinced that Baudelaire, in his last years, converted to Catholicism) but also to Dante, the poet of hope and final redemption.* Finally, just months before his conversion, he read Rimbaud's *Illuminations,* and in September of 1886, *Une Saison en Enfer.* Rimbaud was for Claudel a true "illumination," opening the world of the *surnaturel* to him, so different from that material world about to suffocate him.

His preoccupation with spiritual questions was evident. In August of the same year he had written a poem entitled "Pour la messe des hommes, dernier sacrifice d'amour" in which he speaks of the promise of hope, love, faith, held out by Jesus. But Jesus here is not the son of God. He is a sort of superman of love who,

---

[10] "*Magnificat,*" p. 261.

[11] *Œuvres complètes,* XXV, *Paul Claudel interroge l'Apocalypse,* p. 127.

* In *Mémoires improvisés* Claudel denies that Dante had a religious or literary influence on him, claiming he admired him, but learned little from him. Yet the Beatrice-role of his heroines is striking, as has been remarked upon by more than one critic. See Chapter IV.

through this great power, would definitively save mankind, who can promise "Et vous vivrez toujours, graves et beaux encor." [12] André Vachon in *Le Temps et l'Espace dans l'Œuvre de Paul Claudel* remarks on the resemblance between the Jesus of this poem and Tête d'Or, hero of the play by that name; Tête d'Or also wanted to save men. [13]

Gillet contrasts the conversion of Péguy to that of Claudel. While Péguy approached God slowly, tentatively, even secretly, Claudel's conversion was like a thunderbolt. Writes Gillet, "Nous avons en Claudel l'exemple d'une de ces conversions classiques et absolues, d'une de ces illuminations subites, en un éclair, comme la nuit de Pascal, comme la conversion de son patron Saint Paul ou celle de Saint Augustin." [14] Gillet also points out how differently the two poets envision grace. For Péguy, it is like the dew, gently, insensibly absorbed into the soul. For Claudel it is more often associated with fire, as of course it is in the Bible (v. Acts II: 3). In *l'Annonce* Violaine tells Pierre de Craon to be worthy of the flame that will devour him, and in *Partage de Midi* Mésa and Ysé are finally absolved of their sin in an explosion. Fire purifies Jeanne d'Arc and releases her soul.

Claudel, writing twenty-seven years later, in a much-quoted passage, stresses the lightning-like character of his conversion, telling how he had returned to Notre Dame Christmas evening, casually, as a dilettante who came to enjoy the esthetic beauty of the rites. Without warning, "En un instant mon cœur fut touché et je crus." [15] Analyzing the facts and testimony today, it would seem that his conversion was less sudden than he felt it to be, that it had been preparing from the time of his loss of faith, and that even the black despair which preceded it was part of the preparation, as was also his receptiveness to Rimbaud. But that Christmas 1886 marked the turning point of his life is beyond question.

Returning home that night, Claudel opened a Bible at random, and read two passages to which he would always attach great significance. One was the story of the apostles on the road to Emmaüs,

---

[12] *Œuvre poétique*, "Pour la messe des hommes," p. 6.
[13] André Vachon, *Le Temps et l'Espace dans l'Œuvre de Paul Claudel* (Paris: Ed. du Seuil, 1965), p. 52.
[14] Gillet, p. 20.
[15] *Contacts et Circonstances*, "Ma Conversion," p. 191.

to whom the ressurected Christ appeared; the other, Proverbs, Chapter VIII, in which Wisdom — *la Sagesse* — speaks. Claudel's whole concept of women is intimately bound to *la Sagesse*. It is she who speaks at the end of *l'Esprit et l'Eau* and who warns the poet, "Ne me touchez point! ne cherche pas à prendre ma main," echoing the words of the resurrected Christ to Mary Magdalene (John XX:17). * And in his *Mémoires improvisés* Claudel affirmed, "Pour moi la femme représente toujours quatre choses: soit l'âme humaine, soit l'Eglise, soit la Sainte Vierge, soit la Sagesse sacrée." [16] The role of the woman in Claudel's works is of paramount importance, and is one which I should like to investigate later at greater length, both in connection with the time structure he builds — for the four symbolic values he assigns to her are eternal — and his preference for the Middle Ages, a period when woman, however inferior her socio-economic and political status, was the object of distant veneration — an aspect of courtly love — and religious devotion — as evinced by the cult of the Virgin.

If Claudel's conversion was likely less sudden than he himself realized, it was certainly, and by his own admission, far from complete. A violent spiritual struggle would precede the Christmas of final reconciliation when, in 1890, he made his "second" Communion. "Cette résistance a duré quatre ans. J'ose dire que je fis une belle défense et que la lutte fut loyale et complète. Rien ne fut omis. J'usai de tous les moyens de résistance et je dus abandonner l'une après l'autre des armes qui ne me servaient à rien." [17] During these years he was writing the first version of *Tête d'Or*, a difficult and highly symbolic play which becomes much clearer in meaning if we see it as a metaphor of Claudel's own spiritual battle. In *Mémoires improvisés* Claudel explains his play partly in terms of the adolescent (himself) striking out for independence, looking for new worlds to conquer. But he added, "Au moment où j'ai écrit *Tête d'Or*... je n'avais pas encore fait ma capitulation définitive entre les mains de l'Eglise, et Tête d'Or représente un peu l'espèce de fureur avec laquelle je me défendais contre la Foi qui m'appelait

---

* Only two hours before his death Claudel is reported to have said to his family, "Laissez-moi, laissez moi mourir tranquillement... ne me touchez pas."

[16] *Mémoires improvisés*, p. 51.
[17] *Contacts et Circonstances*, XVI, p. 192.

et qui est symbolisée par la Princesse." [18] The struggle between Simon Agnel (Tête d'Or) * and his invisible foe at the beginning of the play is but one of many symbols of a spiritual battleground.

During this time Claudel was reading Pascal. In "Ma Conversion" he refers to the *Pensées* as a book of inestimable value to those who are searching, but later, in *Mémoires improvisés* he would deny that Pascal had had any real influence, or that he had experienced a comparable anguish. Yet it is hard to miss the Pascalian echoes, or to deny that Tête d'Or is the embodiment of man separated from God. A preoccupation with death and despair before a disordered universe permeates the play. Simon Agnel observes, "Nous avons, à chaque main / une mélancolie désespérée, une noire fable de mystère." [19] Man, removed from God, "cherche en gemissant" and Tête d'Or admits, "J'ai cherché avec angoisse." [20] Cébès, the spiritual half of Tête d'Or, protests the terrible ennui of life:

> Je suis misérable! Puissé-je dire clairement
>   des choses obscures!
> Par où commencerai-je
> Pour exprimer l'ennui qui ne commence pas, mais qui,
>   comme l'objet d'un long regard, reste fixe? [21]

and where Pascal speaks of "un roi dépossédé" Cébès compares himself to "un roi détrôné, revêtu d'habits dérisoires..." [22] Eumère counsels the people, "Souvenez-vous de votre vie affreuse, et rejetant une habitude folle, confiez-vous au pur désespoir." [23] And at the end of the play the centurion pleads with Tête d'Or, "Instruisons-nous ici de désespoir." [24] The critic, Jacques Andrieu (*la Foi dans l'Œuvre de Paul Claudel*) has also recognized and commented on the Pascalian and existential overtones of Claudel's early works. He writes:

---

[18] *Mémoires improvisés*, p. 51.
* Tête d'Or is the epithet Agnel adopts after winning a great battle and saving the Empire.
[19] *Tête d'Or*, I, p. 39.
[20] Ibid., p. 148.
[21] Ibid., p. 40.
[22] Ibid.
[23] Ibid., p. 59.
[24] Ibid., p. 145.

> Toute la psychologie de ces premiers drames... repose sur la représentation de l'âme à la façon d'un vide, d'un creux que l'homme cherche à remplir pas ses accents existentialistes, mais qui n'est autre, au fond, que celle de Pascal expliquant la misère de l'homme par la quête désespérée du divertissement.[25]

Tête d'Or's response is not Christian submission but defiance. If he is indeed a dispossessed king, he will reclaim his possession by sheer will alone. He will kill the Emperor and usurp his place. Rather than accept the world as it is he will wage war on it: "Je tire l'épée contre un monde de pleurs et de fatigue."[26] He dares others to join him in what is essentially a nihilistic challenge: "Qui osera oser? / Et frappant du pied la terre crier: *Je peux!* dans le silence du Néant?" He defies whatever powers there be to do their worst: "Car que peut le chaos même de la nuit de la création / Contre celui dont l'âme, au milieu des ténèbres dans l'oreille même du tourbillon, reste fixe. / Et qui ne craint point la douleur et la mort?"[27]

Tête d'Or is in every sense as much a drama of will as any of Corneille's plays. One is reminded of Auguste's defiance of heaven — "Qu'il joigne à ses efforts le secours des enfers;" and self-affirmation — "Je suis le maître de moi comme de l'univers, / Je le suis, je veux l'être." (*Cinna*, V, iii, vs. 1694-1695). Tête d'Or, too, pits his will, his identity, against the universe. "Le monde, depuis sa création redoutable, / N'est pas assez immense pour m'empecher de dire *Non* si je veux."[28] Against life, death, despair, he opposes his "I." "Combien il est magnifique que cette bouche prononce son Je!"[29] His ambition knows no bounds: "...ne me refusez pas ce que je réclame, qui est Tout,"[30] he tells the people, and when the Emperor rebukes him, he replies, "Tu jalouses ce canton que tu gardes! / Que je saisisse du monde infini, il n'est pas trop petit

---

[25] Jacques Andrieu, *La Foi dans l'Œuvre de Paul Claudel* (Paris: Presses Universitaires de France, 1955), p. 7.
[26] *Tête d'Or,* p. 104.
[27] Ibid., p. 105.
[28] Ibid., p. 98.
[29] Ibid., p. 46.
[30] Ibid., p. 97.

pour moi!"[31] He speaks of his "désir immortel" and it really is just that for he will challenge the gods themselves as their equal opponent. Ultimately, of course, he knows defeat. His will alone has not been enough. At his death he cries, "Je veux, je veux..." and then, "Je ne peux pas! Je ne peux pas! Je ne suis pas un dieu."[32]

In the figure of the Princess we find the symbol of spiritual hope. Who and what is she? At her father's bidding she assumes another identity, and as "Trop Joyeuse" dances for her people. "Qui es-tu donc?" Cébès asks her, then answers his own question, "Tu es notre Gaieté et notre Amour,"[33] and he calls her "Grâce-des-Yeux." The people would not hear her song, and she rebukes them, saying, "Or dirais-je qui je suis?... je suis celle qui élève et nourrit."[34] Speaking of her own martyrdom she presages that of Violaine: "Oh, puissé-je être comme la fleur coupée dont le parfum est plus fort."[35] Questioned about her, Claudel answered indirectly, alluding to the passage in Proverbs where *la Sagesse* speaks. But he also refers to her as the Church, explaining that the first wife (she whom Simon Agnel buries at the beginning of the play) is the "false wife." The true wife — the Princess — is the Church. It is in this role that she struggles for the soul of Tête d'Or:

Je ne permettrai pas que tu meures désespéré. Non, ne crois pas que tu le puisses!
Elle ne t'abandonnera pas, celle que tu as delivrée en baisant ses mains sanglantes!
Voilà que tu as delivré celle qui est plus forte que toi![36]

Tête d'Or's defeat is not total, as Claudel's was not then. He refuses the Princess' consolation, mocks her promise of another life. Yet Claudel hints that, in Tête d'Or's death, the Princess may have won after all. Herself dying, once more dressed in regal splendor, she bestows a gift — her kiss — on his dead body, addressing herself to it: "C'est à toi que je parle, cher corps mort! L'orgueilleux vivant

---

[31] Ibid., p. 96.
[32] Ibid., p. 146.
[33] Ibid., p. 64.
[34] Ibid., p. 64.
[35] Ibid., p. 158.
[36] Ibid., p. 160.

qui t'habitait s'est éloigné avec mépris de toi comme de moi."[37] And Claudel himself, commenting on Tête d'Or's death, remarked, "Toute conversion est une mort plus au moins," adding that his hero, while not explicitly Christian, was perhaps implicitly so.[38]

Tête d'Or not only dramatizes Claudel's spiritual struggle, it foreshadows his mature work. The themes he would later develop and expand are all present in it. In fact, Tête d'Or's defeat is the beginning of victory, for Claudel would and could not accept its finality. Tête d'Or promised the people he would make them "Possesseurs de l'heure Présente" but he failed. Unable alone to overcome time and mortality, Claudel would discover what for him was the true path to the Eternal. Already the Princess was pointing out the direction.

His enormous need to *possess* is really a manifestation of his yearning for immortality (variously represented in his work metaphorical by words like *vide, faim, soif*): "Tu parles du désir, la faim de l'heure présente me tire,"[39] says Tête d'Or, and he seeks to seize the whole world. The desire in itself is not wrong, Claudel would later try to show, only its object. From Tête d'Or's desire to possess a material empire, Claudel would pass to the desire to "possess a soul," — Mésa's, Pierre de Craon's, Orian's (*le Père humilié*) and his own error, and at last to true possession through creative participation in the universe.

Always given to architectural metaphors, Claudel described the intellectual dilemma of his conversion: "L'édifice de mes opinions et de mes connaissances restait debout et je n'y voyais aucun défaut. Il était seulement arrivé que j'en étais sorti."[40] The old building was no longer a suitable home; he would need to construct another. Even as a child in his apple tree he had heard the call of the invisible cathedrals of Laon, Reims, Soissons. Now he would build his own, for "Comment Dieu entrera-t-il dans ton cœur s'il n'y a point de place, / Si tu ne lui fais une habitation? Point de Dieu pour toi sans une église..."[41]

---

[37] Ibid., p. 166.
[38] *Mémoires improvisés*, p. 52.
[39] *Tête d'Or*, p. 80.
[40] *Contacts et Circonstances*, XVI, p. 192.
[41] *La Maison fermée*, p. 283.

In his funeral oration on Claudel's death, Jean Berthoin, Minister of National Education, used the same metaphor, referring to "ce sanctuaire de salubre poésie" that is Claudel's work. "Entre la Terre et le Ciel, il a bâti une sorte de cathédrale aux inebranlables contreforts et dont les tours, bien que se perdant à notre vue, restent toujours à portée d'un élan du cœur." [42]

Claudel's cathedral, his *maison fermée*, is a poetic recreation of the Church Eternal. To begin to understand its construction, it is necessary first to analyze his concept of time and of the poet's creative role, for these two ideas are inextricably linked. His Church "entre la Terre et le Ciel" would be built in a sort of Absolute Present, for as Coeuvre observes in *la Ville*, "Le présent seul existe, étant la superficie de l'éternité permanente." [43]

II

> Tout est joué avant que nous ayons douze ans.
> "Argent"

Charles Péguy was born January 7, 1973, in Orléans, and unlike Claudel, he really did come of peasant stock. His father, Désiré, a carpenter and soldier in the Franco-Prussian war, died just ten months after his son's birth. His mother never remarried. So the child was raised by his grandmother, Etienette Quéré, and his mother, Cécile Péguy, two very formidable women.

On the paternal side, Péguy's family could be traced through parish registers to the 15th century in Orléans, yet he had known none of them. His forebears merged for him into an anonymous mass, "et pourquoi ne pas le dire, il s'enfonce avec orgueil dans cet anonymat. L'anonyme est son patronyme," [44] wrote Péguy of himself.

---

[42] Chaigne, p. 251.
[43] *La Ville*, I, p. 483.
[44] "Note Conjointe sur M. Descartes et la philosophie cartésienne," II, p. 1377.

His grandmother did not come from Orléans, but was born in Gennetines, near Moulins, in the Bourbonnais. Her family was so miserably poor — Péguy refers to them as *gueux* — that she was shunted off to her grandfather. Once he slapped her. "Père grand," she said, "Je ne mangerai plus de votre pain,"[45] and she did not. Although it made a hard life even harder, she preferred to hire herself out as a cowherd to neighboring farmers. Later she learned to make matches, at that time a novelty, and became so adept that she hired other girls to work for her. In 1846 she bore a child, father unknown. Etiennette herself was totally illiterate, but she sent her daughter, Cécile, to school until the little girl was ten.

When the French government prohibited private match production, Etiennette was bought out by the State for a considerable sum. Now without a means of livelihood, she took her daughter and all her possessions, piled them on a raft and floated down the Allier to the Loire and on to Orléans. "Ce fut le temps héroïque," writes Péguy. Without a profession, and too proud to go into the homes of the bourgeoisie, Etiennette took in washing. It was a difficult life at best: "Ma grand'mère garda fièrement la mémoire de ce temps où elle s'était battue toute seule contre la misère elle avait lassé la misère, où malgré la misère elle avait duré..." [sic][46] Péguy declares, a trifle ungrammatical in his admiration.

Péguy's mother, age ten, went to work in a chemical factory, but she soon decided that work was unhealthy. In what her son later regarded as "a stroke of genius" she picked the profession of chair caning, and quickly became so skilled at it that she had a number of private clients. (Péguy admired this profession because it was neither too rough, like laundering, nor too delicate, like lacemaking, but called for both strength and delicacy). With a young son and aging mother to support, it was work, work, *work*. She instilled her respect for honest labor in the young Charles, who developed a sort of reverence for "l'ouvrage bien faite" * which he was never to lose. There was little time for amusements, or displays of affection. Reminiscing about his childhood after her son's death, Madame Péguy affirmed this:

---

[45] "Pierre, Commencement d'une vie bourgeoise," I, p. 1221.
[46] Ibid., p. 1242.
* Péguy uses this phrase often, and always in the feminine, probably an Orléans localism.

> Quand il était petit, — sa chaise sur laquelle il s'asseyait est là près de nous, — je lui faisais faire sa prière du matin et du soir, et il allait à la messe à Saint-Aignan, mais pas avec moi. Moi je n'avais pas le temps, vraiment pas le temps. Nous travaillions dur toutes deux, ma mère et moi, toute la semaine. Le dimanche, on nettoyait. Pensez que je ne me suis seulement jamais promené avec mon Charles, *jamais, jamais, jamais!* [47]

What maternal tenderness the boy received came largely from his grandmother, who took care of him while his mother worked, and passed much of the time telling him stories of her youth. "...elle en savait plusieurs qui étaient amusantes et plusieurs qui étaient merveilleuses; j'aimais mieux celle qui étaient amusante;... j'aimais les histoires merveilleuses, mais j'avais un peu peur qu'elles ne fussent pas vraies." [48] She told the boy how she had cooked soup for her grandfather and taken it out into the forest where he was felling trees. Sometimes, she claimed, she even had to fend off wolves (one suspects this tale belongs in the "histoires merveilleuses" category)!

His mother's philosophy was simple and straightforward: there were two kinds of people, good and bad. Good people were obediant children and good workers; bad people were disobediant children and poor workers. Good workers would surely be recompensed, poor ones would come to an unhappy end. The grown man would ever remain true to this view of life.

Very early he learned to help prepare the cane for his mother, and was pleased when he was able to work faster than his older cousins. "Je commençais de bonne heure à travailler, et cela me faisait un très grand plaisir," he wrote, adding "Je n'aimais pas beaucoup jouer parce que cela n'est pas utile et même n'est guère amusant." [49]

His mother taught him to read and was determined he should go to school. When, at age seven, he entered the *école primaire* *

---

[47] A. Mabille de Poncheville, *Jeunesse de Péguy* (Paris: Alsatia, 1943), p. 31.
[48] "Pierre," p. 1218.
[49] Ibid., p. 1224.

* Péguy also refers to this school as "l'école annexe" because it was annexed to the Ecole normale, where Théodore Naudy was headmaster.

he brought the same industry to his tasks there as to those at home. He rose at six, prepared his lessons, reviewed them during his lunch time, helped cane or delivered finished chairs on his return from school. "Comme écolier, je faisais de mon mieux tout ce que font les écoliers, et comme ouvrier à la maison, quand je n'étais pas encore écolier. J'étais un enfant qui suffisait à deux tâches." [50]

Now the roles of the boy and his grandmother were reversed; it was he who related to her all he had learned in school. But Péguy's new learning did not make him scornful. On the contrary, he admired his grandmother's illiteracy which for him was a positive virtue. Later he would dedicate *La Chanson du Roi Dagobert* to her, "...paysanne qui ne savait lire." In fact, there is in all of Péguy's later work an opposition between *l'esprit* and *la lettre*. In the unfinished "Note Conjointe sur Descartes et la philosophie cartésienne" he explains:

> Dans le silence et l'ombre de l'âme illetrée quelle est donc cette vertu profonde; et surtout quelle est cette grâce profonde? N'est-ce pas la vertu même et la grâce du désarmement de l'ombre...

and he continues:

> ...Comme ce silence et cette ombre sont plus près de la création. Comme ils sont seuls nobles. Comme ils sont seuls près de la création. Tout le reste est industrie. Tout le reste est fatras. Tout le reste est alphabet. [51]

Péguy goes on to compare his own heritage with that of his friend Julien Benda, a Jew. The Jew is a man who has always read, from time immemorial, whereas he, Péguy, has read only since the time of his mother. The "Catholic, Frenchman, peasant," as he characterizes himself, looks into the ranks of his forefathers:

> Derrière sa mère, derrière son père, qu'il n'a pas même connu, cette muraille, cette silencieuse paroi, ce rang de quatre illetrés. Et une parole remonte à l'homme du fond des temps: *La lettre tue.*
>
> *Littera occidet. Littera necat.* [52]

---

[50] Ibid., p. 1239.
[51] "Note Conjointe sur M. Descartes," p. 1302.
[52] Ibid., p. 1383.

The young boy went to a school during the week where he learned about the Republic, and on Sunday, to Saint Aignan, where he learned about God and the great saints of France. There was, he wrote later, no contradiction in his mind. Once a year he watched the re-enactment of Joan of Arc's triumphal entry into Orléans, which originated in his own faubourg de Bourgogne. As a man, Péguy remembered his life in Orléans with much the same nostalgia Claudel looked back on Villeneuve. Both wrote a little elegy for a way of life since vanished. In "Argent" Péguy reminisces:

> Nous avons été élevés dans un tout autre monde. On peut dire dans le sens le plus rigoureux des termes qu'un enfant élevé dans une ville comme Orléans entre 1873 et 1880 a littéralement touché l'ancienne France, l'ancien peuple, le peuple, tout court, qu'il a littéralement participé de l'ancienne France, du peuple. On peut même dire qu'il en a participé entièrement, car l'ancienne France était encore toute, et intacte.[53]

School was to change all this. His mother had modest, bourgeois ambitions for him, and in 1884 sent him to the Ecole professionelle, where he could become a primary school teacher. However, Théodore Naudy, headmaster of the Ecole normale, had already noticed Péguy, and insisted that he enroll in the Lycée d'Orléans at Easter 1885, where he might prepare for a secondary school career. Naudy obtained a scholarship for the boy.

Péguy was twelve in 1885, and the date marks what he felt to be a significant turning point in his life. His mother had already laid out her plans for him. Calling Naudy "l'homme du monde à qui je devais le plus" Péguy explains, "J'étais déjà parti, j'avais déjà dérapé sur l'autre voie, j'étais perdu quand M. Naudy, avec cet entêtement de fondateur, avec cette sorte de rude brutalité qui faisaient vraiment de lui un patron et un maître, réussit à me ressaisir et à me renvoyer en sixième."[54] And again:

> Qui ne s'est assis à la croisée de deux routes. Je me demande souvent avec une sorte d'anxiété rétrospective, avec un vertige en arrière, où j'allais, ce que je devenais, si je

---

[53] "Argent," II, p. 1101.
[54] Ibid., p. 1130.

ne fusse point allé en sixième, si M. Naudy ne m'avait point repêché juste à ces vacances de Pâques. J'avais douze ans et trois mois. Il était temps.[55]

Madame Péguy was not entirely pleased with the abrupt change in career plans. She was a woman always ill-disposed toward interference. She knew "what was best" for her son, expected him to follow her wishes, and even when he was a grown man, tried to exact obediance from him. Jules Isaac give the following, rather frightening description of her:

> Je l'ai bien connue: une femme du peuple, aux idées et aux sentiments simples, élémentaires, formés par la vie la plus dure et le dur travail quotidien, jamais abandonné, même quand, à force d'économiser sou par sou, elle eut acquis une certaine aisance... la mère de Péguy était aussi une maîtresse femme — à la voir on ne pouvait en douter — de grande probité et droiture, mais autoritaire, impérieuse, dure aux autres comme à elle-même, coléreuse, ne supportant pas la moindre résistance à ses volontés, contenant mal la violence d'un tempérament dominateur... Elle savait aimer, certes; comme elle savait aussi détester, haïr! "[56]

It would not be the last time her plans for her son would be frustrated. His later adherence to socialism would infuriate her, for as Roger Sécretain observes in *Péguy, Soldat de la verité*, "Un socialiste, à l'époque, c'était le diable." As for his passionate defense of Dreyfus:

> Dans sa jeunesse, il a eu un moment de folie, comme tous les jeunes gens. L'affaire Dreyfus! Ah! à ce moment-là, il ne m'a pas donné de satisfaction! A ce moment-là il était socialiste, c'est qu'il voulait le bien de l'ouvrier. Mais moi, je me fâchais. Les mamans, ça n'a pas toujours les mêmes idées que les enfants. Il avait vingt-deux ou vingt-trois ans. Il croyait qu'il allait tout retourner. Ah non! je ne voyais pas ça d'un bon œil...[57]

---

[55] Ibid., p. 1131.
[56] Jules Isaac, *Expériences de ma vie* (Paris: Calmann Lévy, 1959), p. 157.
[57] *Jeunesse de Péguy*, p. 42.

Finally, she would be scandalized by Péguy's marriage, which caused him to leave school and abandon a professorial career. She detested his wife, and even more, his mother-in-law. After his death she would often speak nostalgically of his early childhood, "il était si obéissant! Vous savez: rare, comme enfant." [58] Clearly the grown man had not given his mother satisfaction.

Péguy makes two contradictory statements in "Argent." He says that everything is determined by the time we are twelve, and that age twelve was the turning point in his life. Both statements, unhappily for Péguy, were true. For though he was to defy his mother's wishes in regard to both career and marriage, it would only be at great cost to himself. The concept of filial obedience had been so deeply engrained in him in his childhood that whenever he "failed" his mother he suffered deep remorse. It is worth noting here that women dominated both Péguy's real life and his spiritual life as expressed in his poetry. (His mother's possible influence on his work is discussed in Chapter V).

For the first twelve years of Péguy's life there is ample documentation in works like "Argent" and the autobiographical *Pierre*. Less is known about it from the time he entered the Lycée in Orléans until he began to write for the socialist revues in 1897. After completing six years in the Lycée d'Orléans, Péguy, at eighteen, obtained another scholarship, this time to the Lycée de Lakanal at Sceaux, where he could prepare to enter the Ecole normale supérieure and eventually become a university professor. His son, Marcel Péguy, dates his father's loss of faith and his enthusiasm for socialism to that year — 1891 — although Jules Isaac, a fellow student, maintains Péguy attended mass regularly. It is known that he helped collect funds for the striking miners of Carmaux, and perhaps this contact with human misery precipitated a gradual loss of faith in Christianity.

One thing is certain. Péguy disliked Lakanal and failed his entrance exams for the Ecole normale supérieure. Rather than spend a second year at Lakanal, Péguy decided to fulfill his military service requirement. He never wrote about his army experience, but it was apparently a happy one. He enjoyed the comradeship of soldiering

---

[58] Ibid., p. 35.

and ever after looked forward to the annual reserve training period. His poetic heroes would be soldiers as well as saints.

On his release from the army, Péguy again sat for the entrance examinations — and again failed. However, through the good offices of a former professor he obtained a scholarship which allowed him to live at the Collège de Sainte-Barbe while taking courses at the Lycée Louis le Grand.

The twenty year-old student now emerges as an anti-cleric, an unbeliever, and an ardent socialist. Under his leadership a select group of students formed what they called *les amis de la cour rose*. These friendships were to be some of the most lasting and influential in Péguy's life: the Tharaud brothers, renamed by him Jerôme and Jean, Louis Baillet, an idealist like himself, who early chose the Church and became a Benedictine monk, Jules Riby, and a little later, his great friend, Joseph Lotte. The most profound and important bond, however, was that between Péguy and Marcel Baudoin. Little, almost nothing, is known about their relationship which, to judge by the effect of Baudoin's sudden death in 1896, must have been on the level of that which existed between Montaigne and La Boétie. Péguy signed his *Jeanne d'Arc* "Marcel et Pierre Baudoin" although there is no indication Baudoin had collaborated; he also commemorated his friend in the title of his socialist article, "Marcel, Premier dialogue de la Cité harmonieuse." He would later feel it his duty to take his friend's place in the family by marrying Marcel's sister, Charlotte.

The goal of *les amis de la cour rose* was no less than the realization of a socialistic utopia on this earth, beginning with France. But what a peculiar brand of socialism they espoused! Marcel Péguy has attempted to define it: "Mon père avait appelé 'socialisme' une certaine doctrine qui lui était très personnelle... et qui peut se résumer ainsi: socialisme et recherche de la verité sont synonymes." [59] The Tharaud brothers wrote:

> Ce socialisme de Péguy ressemblait beaucoup plus au socialisme de Saint François qu'à celui de Karl Marx. C'était une disposition du cœur, une conception évangélique qui

---

[59] *Lettres et Entretiens*, ed. Marcel Péguy (Paris: Editions de Paris, 1954), p. 24.

venait du fond de son enfance, de la vie qu'il avait menée jusqu'à quinze ou seize ans, à Orléans, rue Bourgogne.[60]

With boundless and naive enthusiasm, the friends expected to have installed all humanity in the "harmonious city" of socialism within forty years! A year later, when Péguy had finally gained admittance to the Ecole normale supérieure, his ardor was undimmed. He and his three study companions carved UTOPIE above the threshold of their *turne*. Yet he was already reading and taking notes for a projected life of Jeanne d'Arc. In 1896 Péguy requested and was granted an extraordinary year's leave of absence, on the pretext that his eyes were bothering him, in actuality, to work on his *Jeanne d'Arc*. Back in Orléans he continued writing (Baudoin read "Domrémy" just before his death), learned typography, took time to found a socialist group.

Returning at the end of 1896 to the Ecole normale to begin his second year, Péguy threw himself into socialist activities, this time formally joining the party. Another strike took place in Carmaux: Péguy rushed to the workers aid, and in the process, met Jean Jaurès. He also came under the influence of Lucien Herr, a rationalist who, as librarian of the Ecole normale, was busy recruiting young socialists.

In February of 1897 his first socialist article appeared in the *Revue Socialiste*. In June of that year he finished his *Jeanne d'Arc*, which was published in December. The most important event of the year, however, was his marriage to Charlotte Baudoin in October. The marriage was apparently contracted by Péguy more out of a sense of duty and loyalty to Marcel than out of love for Charlotte. In any case, it shortly proved to be a very unhappy one, and later Péguy would complain to friends that he felt a stranger within his own family. The Baudoins never forgave him for using all of his wife's dowry to fund his first printing venture, La Librairie de George Bellais, which eventually foundered.

As for Madame Péguy, her fury knew no bounds. Since the marriage forced Péguy to leave school before obtaining his degree, she blamed the Baudoins for aborting a brilliant future. Jules Isaac reports:

---

[60] Jérome et Jean Tharaud, *Notre cher Péguy*, II (Paris: Plon, 1926), p. 18.

> L'entrée de Péguy dans la famille Baudouin, son mariage et toutes les conséquences qu'il avait entraînées — départ de l'Ecole, fondation de la librairie — avaient déchaîné les foudroyantes colères maternelles. L'échec de Péguy à l'agrégation de philosophie en 1898, échec inévitable, acheva d'exaspérer la mère. Bien entendu, la jalousie féminine tenait sa place dans la querelle, et l'on sait qu'elle est communément sans merci d'une femme à l'autre — ou aux autres. C'était le cas Péguy-Baudoin. La mère de Péguy en voulait furieusement à sa bru, et plus encore à l'autre mère, Mme Baudoin, la belle-mère. Le conflit devint tel que Péguy lui-même s'en effrayait, tremblait à l'idée d'affronter celle à laquelle il devait tant et si longtemps s'était exercé à obéir docilement, pieusement.[61]

In spite of (or perhaps, because of) his personal problems, Péguy plunged ever more deeply into socialist activities. When the Dreyfus affair exploded in January 1898 with Zola's famous "*J'accuse...*" Péguy joined the battle as a Dreyfusard. To him it was a simple case of right and wrong. Dreyfus was innocent: there could not be any other consideration.

Péguy's early socialist writings are most important in understanding the development of his thought, and even though they follow it, shed light on the *Jeanne d'Arc*. For in his life, unlike in that of Claudel, there is no clear-cut turning point. His conversion would come much later, when he was a mature man of thirty-five. Yet, as a Christian, he never renounced anything he had written earlier. His thought seemed to develop in ever-widening but concentric circles, from socialism through Bergsonism and finally to Christianity. There is an integrity — and I give the word its full etymological value, in both his interior and exterior life that is truly extraordinary. Perhaps more than any modern writer Péguy, to borrow Montaigne's self-description, "marche tout d'une pièce."

Juarès and Herr had high hopes for the young radical, yet his first writings should have forewarned them. "De la cité socialiste" is plainly the work of an impractical visionary. Péguy begins with the socialist axiom that suffering is chiefly caused by an inequitable distribution of wealth, and must be solved through a socialized state. But, although production would be pooled, people would be

---
[61] Isaac, p. 157.

entirely free to choose their occupations according to desire and ability. There would be no demeaning work. If a certain task held little appeal the workers who undertook it would be compensated by shorter hours, and if that inducement were not enough the work would be made "compulsory and universal and personal." (In practical terms this apparently meant that everyone might have to dispose of his own garbage.)

Péguy returned to the subject a year later, in "Marcel, Premier dialogue de la cité harmonieuse," where he described "La cité dont nous préparons la naissance et la vie." [62] Everyone would be a welcome citizen of the harmonious city, and typically, he itemizes: Greek, Jew, Aryan, Latin, German, Slav, all cultures, philosophies and religions, not forgetting the animals. Péguy remains true to his mother's precepts: "La cité harmonieuse, pour assurer sa vie corporelle, travaille." [63] In fact, the work assures the harmony. Only the young, the fit, the male shall work, for work entails responsibility, and it would not be right for the old, infirm, adolescents or women to be responsible for the city. (The animals, incidentally, would not work "parce que les animaux sont des âmes adolescentes"). [64] Although jobs would differ according to ability and need, they would be equal: that is, those who commanded were not to be regarded as superior, but only as people whose job it was to command. Masters would be good masters; apprentices, good apprentices.

The inhabitants of the harmonious city would be different, too. Among them there would be no seeking of fame, no rivalry: "En la cité harmonieuse, toutes les âmes collectives naissent et croissent libres et pures en force et selon la beauté qui leur est personnelle." [65] They would not "remember" those sentiments which tear apart the fabric of modern society — hate, public or private ambitions, vengeance, etc. In short, "Ils ne savent pas ce que c'est le mensonge." [66] Artistic life would flourish. Artists and philosophers would not be required to contribute to the material life of the city, but only to

---

[62] "Marcel: Premier dialogue de la Cité harmonieuse," I, p. 11.
[63] Ibid., p. 13.
[64] Ibid., p. 12.
[65] Ibid., p. 42.
[66] Ibid., p. 43.

nourish within themselves and finally produce the beauty they see, that through creation, it might be shared by all the inhabitants.

Given such an idealistic vision, together with Péguy's own uncompromising nature, it was hardly surprising that this "socialist" who constituted his own majority of one should break with the party. Péguy was totally disillusioned by the resolutions passed by the Socialist Congress in 1898 forbidding internal criticism, and characteristically refused to accept the edict. Without funds, married, now a father (his son, Marcel, had been born in September 1898), he would nevertheless undertake to publish "le journal vrai," with the most unimaginative — almost childish — title of *Les Cahiers de la Quinzaine*. In the first series of the first *Cahier* Péguy made his readers a promise he was to keep: "Dire la vérité, toute la vérité, rien que la vérité, ennuyeusement la vérité ennuyeuse, tristement la vérité triste."[67] Marcel Péguy had good reason for identifying his father's socialism with his search for truth.

In "Marcel" Péguy depicted life as he would have liked it to be: in *Jeanne d'Arc* he showed it as it really was, with all its attendant suffering, poverty, and lies. And what a jolt this book must have been to his socialist friends (at least to those who bothered to read it)! Here, at the height of the Dreyfus affair, when socialism and anticlericalism were synonymous, Péguy, in a mixture of prose and poetry, was writing of voices, visions, saints and martyrs.

To the author there was no contradiction, for Jeanne was a socialist after his own inclination. As the Tharaud brothers point out:

> Cette fille d'une audace ingénue, qui ne tenait compte de rien, ni des obstacles matériels, ni des autorités régulières, qui refusait de se soumettre à l'expérience des capitaines, aux conseils des politiques, aux avertissements des gens d'Eglise, bref qui n'obéissait qu'à son inspiration profonde, représentait à ses yeux toutes les dispositions de l'esprit et du cœur qu'il fallait apporter dans la lutte sociale pour que la bataille fût gagnée. Le temps ne faisait rien. Jean restait le type du héros socialiste, et tout simplement du héros.[68]

---

[67] "Lettre du provincial," I, p. 94.
[68] Tharaud, pp. 107-108.

The task which Péguy and his friends of the *cour rose* had set for themselves, that of converting all France and after it the world to socialism within forty years, was no less formidable or quixotic than that which faced the Maid of Orléans. Moreover, in Péguy's thought, socialism was intimately linked with the heroic traditions of France. Looking back on those early years at Sainte-Barbe and the Ecole normale in "Notre Jeunesse" he characterizes his socialism in a long (here, abridged) paragraph remarkable for the absence of verbs:

> Ai-je besoin de dire, pour mémoire, de noter et de faire noter combien ce socialisme même était dans la pure tradition française, combien il était dans la ligne, dans la lignée française ... Dans la sève et la race même ... un héroïsme enfin plein et sobre, gai et discret, un héroïsme à la française. [69]

Jeanne embodies this heroism, an appositive in Péguy's grammar as in his mind, of socialism.

She is poor, and this poverty is a necessary, not accidental quality. As a child, Péguy had respected poverty,* as a socialist he distrusted wealth, and later as a Christian he would come to see a direct correlation between poverty and sanctity: "... il y a une affinité, une parenté infiniment profonde et qui va infiniment loin entre le christianisme et l'organique (la *vie* éternelle) et la pauvreté." [70]

Like his own grandmother, Jeanne is unlettered. When she wants to make a final appeal to the English before going into battle, she must dictate it, affixing a simple cross by her name. As we have seen, Péguy respected this peasant ignorance which he equated with innocence. As the good king Dagobert observes, "Vaillant soldat du roi / Ne doit signer que par sa croix." [71]

---

[69] "Notre Jeunesse," I, p. 605.

* M. Saint-Clair has gone so far as to attribute Péguy's peculiar style to his childhood poverty: "Il faut être pauvre pour regarder les choses avec cette piété, ce respect, cette volonté de profit, pour inventorier avec ce soin ... Le style de Péguy portera la marque de cette habitude de pauvre, c'est un pli ineffable. Il n'abandonnera jamais rien, il ne trouvera rien à ne pas dire." *Galerie privée*, "Charles Péguy" (Paris: Gallimard, 1947), p. 169.

[70] "Clio, Dialogue de l'Histoire et de l'Ame païenne," II, p. 131.

[71] *La Chanson du Roi Dagobert*, O.P., p. 359.

Most importantly, Jeanne is a good worker. A faithful shepherdess, she delays her departure until morning because someone must look after the sheep that night. How often during the campaigns she longs for the simple and satisfying tasks on her father's farm. To a soldier from Lorraine she confides, "Ah, maître Jean, comme ils sont heureux, ceux qui sont en Lorraine, et comme il ferait bon filer encore la laine en gardant les moutons dans les près de la Meuse." When maître Jean reminds her that one must do ones work where it is found, she sadly agrees: "Vous avez raison, mon maître: il faut qu'on travaille chacun de son métier tant qu'on trouve de l'ouvrage. Voici quels sont les ordres pour aujourd'hui..."[72] Or again, when Madame Jacqueline attempts to keep Jeanne's officers from disturbing her prayer, the latter gently rebukes her: "...à présent, quand on viendra me trouver pour la besogne, il ne faudra pas avoir peur de me déranger, même dans la prière, parce que, voyez-vous, travailler à la besogne, c'est encore de la prière."[73] Péguy, professed unbeliever, wrote these lines. After his conversion he would say the same thing, recalling the remark peasants used to make just to annoy their curé: "Travailler, c'est prier." This ethic of work, acquired in childhood, is intimately bound up in Péguy's concept of socialism, with his idea of *ancienne France,* and finally, with Christian values. Jeanne's pride of workmanship will not permit her to leave a task unfinished. After her defeat at the gates of Paris a priest tries to persuade her that her work is finished and that she should return home. She replied, "Non, mon père, je n'irai pas chez moi, me reposer, tant que mon œuvre ne sera point parfaite."[74]

One of Jeanne's greatest strengths is her attachment to French soil. Her ancestors, like Péguy's own, merge into an anonymous mass who have served, nevertheless, to preserve the continuity of French greatness. Jeanne takes leave of the Meuse very much as Péguy must have left the Loire he loved:

> Adieu, Meuse endormeuse et douce à mon enfance,
> Qui demeures aus prés, où tu coules tout bas.

---

[72] *Jeanne d'Arc,* O.P., p. 162.
[73] Ibid., p. 113.
[74] Ibid., p. 200.

> Meuse, adieu: j'ai déjà commencé ma partance
> En des pays nouveaux où tu ne coules pas. [75]*

It is a sustained and moving song of farewell. Then Jeanne bids goodbye to her home, "maison de pierre forte... maison fidèle et calme à la prière," a home which in Péguy's imagination must have resembled the cottage in the faubourg de Bourgogne.

The Tharauds were correct in saying that Jeanne symbolized not just the socialist hero, but the Hero, pure and simple. She is in the long tradition of French chivalry. At the time he wrote the first *Jeanne d'Arc* Péguy's favorite play was *Polyeucte,* and it would always remain so. He admired the rivalry between the Christian, Polyeucte, and the Stoic, Sévère, which he thought of as a duel in the tradition of the *chansons de geste,* a duel between worthy opponents who would have preferred honorable defeat to dishonorable victory. Jeanne is such a combatant. She refuses to attack the English until she has given them a chance to withdraw voluntarily, because, "Il ne faut jamais commencer la guerre avant d'avoir essayé le paix." [76] The means are every bit as important as the end. She needs soldiers who can kill and be killed without damning their souls or those of their victims to hell, for without a "good" army how can she fight a "good" war? When the cynical Gilles de Rais tells her that instead of talking to the troops about God, saints, France, and peace she should describe the booty and woman awaiting them in Paris, Jeanne is saddened. "S'il fallait, pour sauver la France, prononcer les paroles que monsieur de Rais a prononcées devant moi... j'aimerais mieux... que la France ne fût pas sauvée." [77] This idea of the just war, almost intuitive in the early *Jeanne,* would be developed at greater length and with much more precision in Péguy's later works, becoming an integral part of his whole system of thought.

---

* This poem along with other excerpts from the drama was set to music in a sort of symphonic poem by Maurice Jaubert who, like Péguy, was killed in battle (in 1940). The recorded performance, unfortunately, is not commercially available.

[75] Ibid., p. 80.
[76] Ibid., p. 69.
[77] Ibid., p. 173.

When Péguy first envisioned his work, he had planned a carefully documented historical portrait, and it is, in fact, historically accurate.* But as he proceeded he became more and more interested in Jeanne's inner life as opposed to the events in her exterior or historical life. It was to explore the former that he decided to exploit the resources of dramatic and poetic media. The resulting dichotomy is one of the play's defects. The historian of the exterior life succeeds the poet of the inner life. When Péguy took up the subject twelve years later, he would correct this defect. *Le Mystère de la Charité de Jeanne d'Arc* would concern itself uniquely with Jeanne's inner life, and only the voice of the poet would be heard.

In many ways Jeanne represents her creator. The critic, Lucien Christophe, whose work, *Le Jeune Péguy,* centers around the early years of Péguy, saw in *Jeanne d'Arc* an attempt by the poet to give substance through it to all the remembered beauty of his childhood: "Le *Jeanne d'Arc* de Péguy est l'œuvre d'un poète qui a voulu donner un corps aux émotions de son enfance et de son adolescence et recréer une figure de gloire et de beauté en se fiant à ses voix à lui, les voix de la colère, les voix de la fidélité, les voix de l'espérance." [78]

Not only did Péguy give Jeanne many of his own memories and childhood joys, but, on the debit side, his spiritual problems. As his hero Tête d'Or reflected the young Claudel's religious dilemma, so Jeanne's inner life mirrors the despair of Péguy — the Pascalian anguish of man separated from God.

It may seem curious to speak of despair in connection with a man who worked so tirelessly and apparently so confidently to attain his Utopia, and who, with *Le Porche de la deuxième vertu,* would become the apostle of Hope. But the word is exact. In fact, Hope became for him the most precious of the three virtues precisely because it was the most difficult for him to practice.

Jeanne is tortured by the useless suffering she sees around her. In the very first scene we learn that she has shared her bread with

---

* In 1894 and 1895 Péguy is known to have read, as well as Michelet, the *Histoire de Charles VII* by Vallet de Vireville, Wallon's *Jeanne d'Arc,* and that of Lanery d'Arc, the five-volume *Procès de Jeanne d'Arc* by Quichérat, and the latter's *Aperçus nouveaux sur l'histoire de Jeanne d'Arc.*

[78] Lucien Christophe, *Le Jeune Homme Péguy* (Brussels: Renaissance du Livre, 1964), p. 39.

two orphans, but takes no consolation from the act because she knows tomorrow they will be hungry again. Like his heroine, Péguy could not tolerate the misery he saw around him. In the important article, "Encore de la grippe," written in 1900 during a bout with serious illness, he expressed his distress: "L'Europe est malade, la France est malade. Je suis malade. Le monde est malade." [79]

Yet neither Péguy nor Jeanne surrender to despair. Both *act*. When Jeanne is asked at her trial why she did not simply content herself with prayers for a French victory, she replies, "C'est une habitude en France, quand on voit qu'on a du travail à faire, de commencer par essayer d'y travailler soi-même." [80] Looking to some distant source of help is dangerous because it paralyzes. When Hauviette reminds Jeanne that the dauphin is seeking aid from Scotland she answers, "Justement: c'est trop loin, l'Ecosse. Le secours de la France, il est en France." [81] In "Encore de la grippe," much of which is devoted to a discussion of Pascal, Péguy criticizes the latter and Christians in general because their hope for the next world makes them turn away from the problems of this world. "Je ne suis pas très partisan des speculations immenses, des contemplations éternelles," he tells his doctor. "Je n'ai pas le temps. Je travaille par quinzaines. Je m'attache au présent. Il en vaut la peine ... Je travaille dans les misères du présent." [82]

Jeanne not only suffers from the material evil she sees: she is obsessed by the idea of damnation. And here we have the most probable explanation of Péguy's own loss of faith. He simply could and would not accept the idea of a God who would damn any soul eternally. This is Jeanne's dilemma, too. She would save not only France but all the tortured souls in Hell.

> O s'il faut, pour sauver de la flamme éternelle
> Les corps des morts damnés s'affolant de souffrance,
> Abandonner mon corps à la flamme éternelle;
>
> *un silence*
>
> Et s'il faut, pour sauver de l'Absence éternelle
> Les âmes des damnés s'affolant de l'Absence,

---

[79] "Encore de la grippe," I, p. 157.
[80] *Jeanne d'Arc*, p. 269.
[81] Ibid., p. 62.
[82] "Encore de la grippe," p. 156.

> Abandonner mon âme l'Absence éternelle,
> Que mon âme s'en aille en l'Absence éternelle. [83]

Péguy even attributes this anguish — his own and his heroine's — to the dying Christ:

> Etant le Fils de Dieu, Jésus connaissait tout
> Et le Sauveur savait que ce Judas, qu'il aime,
> Il ne le sauvait pas, se donnant tout entier.
>
> Et c'est alors qu'il sut la souffrance infinie,
> C'est alors qu'il sentit l'infinie agonie
> Et clama comme un fou l'épouvantable angoisse,
> Clameur dont chancella Marie encor debout,
>
> Et par pitié du Père il eut sa mort humaine. [84]

Jeanne's last prayer is not for herself, but for the salvation of all: "Pourtant, mon Dieu, tâchez donc de nous sauver tous, mon Dieu. / Jésus, sauvez-nous tous à la vie éternelle." [85]

Both Tête d'Or and Jeanne are in revolt. Both have a messianic desire to *save*, although Tête d'Or's desire takes a nihilistic form. At the time of writing, neither author had found a satisfactory means of action, and that is why both plays end on an equivocal note. Tête d'Or dies, broken but unrepentent; Jeanne's last prayer, her use of the verb *tâcher*, shows her uncertainty, even at the moment of death. This revolt and uncertainty notwithstanding, Claudel and Péguy reveal, through their early works, that each, rejecting despair, intends to take action. If the world as they found it was unacceptable to both men, it remains to be seen how they would — to use Claudel's terminology — recreate it, or — to use Péguy's — build the Harmonious City.

---

[83] *Jeanne d'Arc*, p. 38.
[84] Ibid., p. 39.
[85] Ibid., p. 326.

CHAPTER II

TIME

> Nous ne sommes plus avec le temps, nous sommes avec la source du temps.
>
> *Un Poète regarde la Croix*

In his moment of illumination Claudel received absolute faith, but as he admitted, the edifice of his intellectual beliefs had been left intact, and he could see no flaw in it. Since that building could no longer serve him as a residence, however, he would be forced to construct another. It is in *Art Poétique,* composed of three essays (*Connaissance du temps,* 1903; *Traité de la Co-naissance,* 1904; *Développement de l'Eglise,* 1900) that he builds the intellectual structure which can house his belief in God and in eternal life. And it is in *Les Cinq Grandes Odes* that the theories developed in *Art Poétique* find their clearest, perhaps most remarkable application.

In writing *Art Poétique* Claudel was responding to a deep-felt personal need. In a letter to Gabriel Frizeau he confided to his friend, "Mon dernier ouvrage [*Traité de la Co-naissance*] m'a soulagé d'un grand doute qui ne me laissait pas de repos depuis longtemps, sur l'état de notre connaissance après la mort."[1] In *Développement de l'Eglise* he speaks of the symbolic important of the roof: "La toiture est l'invention purement de l'homme qui a besoin que soit complète la clôture de cette cavité pareille à celle de la tombe et du ventre maternel qu'il réintègre pour la réfection du sommeil et de la nourriture."[2] Thus Claudel believed that this need for "clô-

---

[1] *Art poétique,* p. 209.
[2] *Correspondance,* Claudel, Jammes, Frizeau, p. 57.

ture" was not peculiar to him, but universal. Man wants a "closed house." In other words, there is in him a desire for permanence which — and this is one aspect of existential absurdity — is continually frustrated by the transitory nature of the human condition and the inevitability of his own death.

The new house was a long time abuilding, as evinced by the violence of the struggle in *Tête d'Or,* and the fact that he did not even partake of Holy Communion until Christmas of 1890. To understand how he went about its construction — where he got his "lumber" — it is important to know what Claudel was reading. For, despite his scorn for "intellectuals," his intellectual and spiritual life are virtually inseparable — the reason, of course, that he needed a new intellectual edifice in the first place.

In the two years following his illumination he was deep into Pascal's *Pensées,* Dante's *Divine Comedy,* and Aristotle's *Metaphysics.* We have already noted echoes of pascalian anguish in *Tête d'Or,* and the Princess in that play is certainly a Beatrice figure. Aristotle's influence would be felt in *Art Poétique.* Claudel's confessor, the abbot Villaume, suggested he seek spiritual guidance in St. Thomas Aquinas. For three years Claudel studied the latter's writings, with the result that Thomist thought is at the very bases of *Art Poétique.*

The year he wrote *Développement de l'Eglise,* 1900, was a particularly painful one to Claudel, in which he knew both divine rejection and human renunciation. He had longed to enter the Benedictine order, but after a stay with the monks, first at Solesmes, then at Ligugé, he received what he felt was a clear "no" from God. No reason given, just *no.* Against his will he would have to continue his double career as writer-diplomat. In the same year he wrote the first section of the first of his *Cinq Grandes Odes, Les Muses.* I have said that the odes represent the application of the esthetic theories of *Art Poétique.* They also mirror his spiritual and emotional conflicts, his rebellion, and final submission.

Stung by God's unexplained rejection, he departed for a mission in China. On the long sea voyage he met a young — and married — Polish woman with whom he fell deeply in love (and whose identity has been concealed to the present writing). So intense was the involvement that when Claudel externalized his feelings in *Partage de Midi* (1905) he allowed only a few copies to be printed for distribution among close friends, and the play was not released (in edited form) for general publication until 1948. The necessity and pain of renunciation is an important theme in the odes which follow *Les Muses*, especially in *L'Esprit et l'Eau* and *La Muse qui est la Grâce*.

In March 1906 — and possibly because he had externalized his love in *Partage de Midi* — Claudel married Reine Sainte-Marie Perrin. The couple left immediately for China, and it was from Peking that Claudel wrote *L'Esprit et l'Eau*. A year later his wife presented him with his first child, appropriately named Marie, and the poet produced the *Magnificat* and *La Muse qui est la Grâce*. Finally, in 1908 he was able to entitle his last ode, *La Maison Fermée*.

With this poem, construction of Claudel's new spiritual and intellectual home was finished. It had taken twelve years to complete, and the youth of eighteen was a mature man of thirty.

Before the new can be built the old must be razed. And that is precisely how Claudel began. As he wrote to Gide:

> Ma grande joie est de penser que nous assistons au crépuscule de la Science du XIXe siècle. Toutes ces abominables théories qui ont opprimé notre jeunesse, celle de Laplace; celle de l'évolution, celle des équivalents de force, s'écroulent d'une sur l'autre. Nous allons enfin respirer à plain poumons la sainte nuit, la bienheureuse ignorance... Quelle absurdité, quand on y réfléchit, de prétendre jamais expliquer quoi que ce soit, de prétendre à l'épuiser en tant que source de connaissance alors que le nombre des accords d'où naît celle-ci est infini! Je compose en ce moment une espèce de poème dialectique pour célébrer l'avènement des temps nouveaux et cette délectable ignorance...[3]

The very first thing Claudel does in *Connaissance du Temps*, his "espèce de poème dialectique," even before discussing the nature of time itself, is to demolish the idea of any operative determinism in the world. Just as Péguy would do, he restores the variety and spontaneity of life. The determinists, he says, would have us believe that for every case there is an effect, and this effect is predictable,

---

[3] *Correspondance*, Claudel, Gide, p. 48.

ensuing from the operation of certain "laws." This, says Claudel, is not so. "L'une n'est rattachée à l'autre par aucune nécessité logique."[4] With the benefit of hindsight, one can give the cause of Napoleon's defeat as the Russian winter, but one could not have predicted such an effect, the infinite possibilities of life being such that the confrontation of the Grande Armée and the Russian winter might have had quite other outcomes. "Les choses ne sont point comme les pièces d'une machine, mais comme les éléments en travail inépuisable d'un dessin toujours nouveau," and he tells the determinists, "Où vous suivez la marche d'une *machine,* je goûte la pratique d'un instrument. Il n'y a point de lois, il n'y a que des *recettes.*"[5]

Having reaffirmed the multiplicity of life, Claudel now turns to the definition of time. Here his philosophic argument is clearly based on the thought structure of St. Thomas. Time, according to Aquinas, is motion. Every living thing is a mixture of Being and Becoming: he acts and he is acted upon, changed, moved. This susceptibility St. Thomas calls *potentia*. Only God has no *potentia*: he is *actus purus,* therefore motionless, therefore eternal. Other living things, in descending order as they act or are acted upon, exist only by analogy to God, and by their limited participation in Him. The final goal of the soul, which cannot be attained in this life, is the Beatific Vision, the moment when the soul will comprehend the total order of the universe and its causes. Time itself will cease to exist, and the soul will participate in the Eternal. It is just such a Beatific Vision that Claudel is approaching in *Art Poétique*. He begins with the TIME = MOTION equation. For example, the movement of the planets is "l'inscription du temps dans l'espace,"[6] or again, "...l'heure, inscrite sur l'émail ou le calendrier, marque la position commune des choses dans la durée."[7] In fact, because of the identity of time and motion, the whole universe is one gigantic clock, "...si le mouvement et le temps sont les expressions homologues d'un même fait, il suit que tout mobile animé de l'un sert

---

[4] *Art poétique,* p. 131.
[5] Ibid., p. 133.
[6] Ibid., p. 137.
[7] Ibid., p. 142.

à indiquer l'autre et fait partie de l'entière machine chronométrique." [8]

Time, being movement, is the direction or sense of life, and here Claudel elaborates to give the latter term every possible shade of meaning: "Le temps est le *sens* de la vie. (*Sens*: comme on dit le sens d'un cours d'eau, le sens d'une phrase, le sens d'une étoffe, le sens de l'odorat.)" [9]

Now, according to Scholastic thinking, *matter* changes, *form* does not. Correspondingly, there is the passing hour, imprisoned in a watch case which "ne laisse pour effet de son passage qu'une certaine fatigue du ressort," and there is "l'heure totale, créatrice." [10] Claudel explains this distinction:

> Cependant à toute heure de la Terre il est toutes les heures à la fois; à chaque saison, toutes les saisons ensemble. Pendant que l'ouvrière en plumes voit qu'il est Midi du cadran de la Pointe-Saint-Eustache, le soleil de son premier rayon ras troue la feuille Virginienne, l'escadre des cachalots sur la Poméranie, pendant que le Paraguay n'est que roses, pendant que Melbourne grille. Il semble que ce qui existe ne puisse jamais cesser d'être, et que du temps destiné à traduire l'existence sous le mode passager, chaque partie ayant, comme nous l'avons dit une forme concrète et sa figure comme une femme, comporte une nécessité, permanente, inéluctable. [11]

It is almost as if Claudel, once more in his apple tree at Villeneuve, could "englobe" the earth in his vision.

There is, in Claudel's notion of time, both repetition and constant renewal: "Demain, sur le cercle des chiffres, la même ligne annoncera Minuit. Et sur le cadran même de la Terre d'un an à l'autre Juillet se définit par des traits semblables. Jamais pourtant il n'est pas le même juillet. Sous les rythmes fermés du jour et de la saison, il est une heure absolue . . ." [12] Time, one can say, is generative: "Le passé est la condition sans cesse grossie du future, l'éternelle

---

[8] Ibid., p. 138.
[9] Ibid., p. 135.
[10] Ibid., p. 139.
[11] Ibid.
[12] Ibid., p. 142.

proposition créatrice de la tonique à la dominante." [13] TIME = MOTION and time creates. Therefore, since man is mobile (i.e., he *lives*) then TO LIVE = TO CREATE.

This extraordinarily dynamic idea of time leads to a contemplation of the present, which is always new. Physical forces and human will cooperate in the making of what Claudel calls *le mosaïque Instant.* "La minute présente diffère de toutes les autres minutes en ce qu'elle n'est pas la lisière de la même quantité de passé. Elle n'explique pas le même passé, elle n'implique pas le même futur." [14] And he concludes joyfully, "A chaque trait de notre haleine, le monde est aussi nouveau qu'à cette première gorgée d'air dont le premier homme fit son premier souffle." [15]

In the conclusion of *Connaissance du Temps* Claudel speaks of time as movement *from* rather than *toward,* as an *invitation to die*: "Le temps est le moyen offert à tout ce qui sera d'être afin de n'être plus." [16] This conclusion, however, which emphasized death, could not have been satisfactory. There is indeed a *push,* or movement *from* God and toward the temporal, but there is also a *pull* toward Him and the eternal. Our course, perfected in the divine mind, is circular, and finally leads us back to God. This modification of the conclusion of the earlier essay is spelled out in the second part of *Art Poétique,* entitled in full *Traité de la Co-naissance au monde et de soi-même.*

In the *Traité* Claudel explores the whole question of the relation of the temporal to the eternal world, and man's situation in regard to both. *Nous ne naissons pas seuls. Naître, pour tout, c'est connaître.* These two opening sentences both announce the subject of discussion and summarize it. Man can only know and define himself by *what he is not,* that is, in terms of the world around him. Through his senses he comes into contact with that world, through his reason he assimilates the messages of his senses. Thus simultaneously he is born with (il co-naît) and he knows (il connaît).

There is, as St. Thomas had insisted, an ascending ladder of life, from mineral to vegetable to man. (Animals, incidentally, fare poorly with Claudel. Like Descartes, he regards them as "machines,"

---

[13] Ibid., p. 145.
[14] Ibid., p. 140.
[15] Ibid.
[16] Ibid., p. 145.

where as for Péguy they were co-habitants in the Harmonious City and "des âmes adolescentes.") All forms of life share one, and only one universal quality, and that is movement. But man differs from animals in that he is "general" whereas they are "particular." To illustrate: an animal, being hungry, may find food in the fruit of a certain tree. It will "remember" that tree, and return to it later, but only when motivated by hunger. Man, on the contrary, does not need any particular stimulus to relate to another being or thing. "Il est capable de trouver partout sa place, de réaliser sa forme à l'égard de toute chose à l'état de différence et de co-naître selon elle."[17] He is able to generalize and to think abstractly, and it is by this ability that he not only assimilates but dominates the world around him. For the essence of abstraction, and that which sets man apart from other animals, is the word. "Je deviens maître, avec le mot, de l'objet qu'il représente, je puis le transporter où je veux avec moi, je puis faire comme s'il était là. Nommer une chose, c'est la répéter en court; c'est substituer au temps qu'elle met à être celui que nous prenons à l'énoncer."[18] Moreover, there is an interrelationship (a *co-naissance*) between man, naming ... thinking ... and the object named.

> Le mot n'est pas seulement la formule de l'objet. Il est l'image de moi-même en tant qu'informé par cet objet. Quand je pense "le chien," ce que je fais, c'est moduler aussitôt, disposer les différentes images et impressions dont cet animal est le support. Quand je dis, "le chien aboie," c'est le chien dans la pensée qui aboie, ce chien assimilé à qui j'impartis mon énergie de sujet; je répète en court l'action, j'en deviens moi-même l'auteur, l'acteur.[19]

This is the dynamic aspect of man. Not only does he dominate through the word, but he "becomes." "Sous les coups de l'énergie qu'il dirige, il se modèle et reforge sa personne."[20]

Claudel develops the Rimbaldean mystique of the word within a Christian context. He explores what Valéry called "the poetic state" and the role of the poet. When matter (Animus) comes into

---

[17] Ibid., p. 174.
[18] Ibid., p. 178.
[19] Ibid., p. 179.
[20] Ibid., p. 191.

contact with spirit (Anima) it experiences a sort of shuddering, or vibration. "La vibration de notre cervelle est le bouillonnement de la source de la vie, l'émotion de la matière au contact de l'unité divine..." [21] This divine impulse acts like a shock: it must be elaborated, transmitted. God gives man the word so that man can return it to him in praise. "Et voici que la vie a tresailli dans son sein... Se connaître, pour lui, c'est se faire co-naître, se fournir comme moyen de co-naissance, c'est faire naître par soi, avec soi, tous les objets dont il a connaissance." [22] Through the word, man creates. Thus, as the word imitates the Word, so man imitates his Creator, and himself partakes of the divine nature. [23]

In the fifth and final section of the *Traité* Claudel considers the state of the soul after death. Then at last shall the soul behold the Beatific Vision. But — and this is important — even before his death man can, for a fleeting, privileged moment, glimpse that vision:

> Et cependant, même en ce monde périssable... l'éternité, sous sa forme circulatoire, ne présente à l'esprit rien que de facile et de familier; nous ne pouvons de rien dire qu'il commence ou finit. Nous voyons demeurer des cadres fixes que remplit une matière en mouvement. L'idée d'éternité se réduit à celle d'une *fermeture* par elle-même, et nous avons vu que rien en ce monde n'échappe à la nécessité de la forme. Lors le Temps sera fermé sur nous et le Présent en sera le centre éternel. [24]

Time will be closed around an absolute, eternal Present, and "notre occupation pour l'éternité sera l'accomplissement de notre part dans la perpétration de l'Office." [25]

It is clear from the conclusion of the *Traité de la Co-naissance* that Claudel's idea of time is based upon liturgical time, that is, its movement is not linear but circular, and it revolves about an absolute present, *l'Heure*. In his most interesting book, *Le Temps et l'Espace dans l'Œuvre de Paul Claudel*, André Vachon points up the tremendous importance of both the liturgical year and the ca-

---

[21] Ibid., p. 161.
[22] Ibid., p. 186.
[23] Ibid., p. 194.
[24] Ibid., p. 204.
[25] Ibid.

nonical hours in the works of Claudel. Vachon insists upon Claudel's need to find the *center* of time and space alike: the center of Pierre de Craon's rose church; or Rome, and within it, St. Peter's Cathedral, center of the spiritual world. In time, the privileged hours are Noon and Midnight which divide the day but belong to neither part — which simply *are*. He points out the voluntary confusion between the festival of Easter — the hour of Resurrection, hence the center — and Christmas. Vachon observes that at the end of *La Ville,* though we are told it is Holy Saturday before Easter, the stars are described in a position they would only hold in late December. Certainly this superposition applies as well to *l'Annonce faite à Marie* when, through Violaine's mediation (a virgin "birth") and at Christmas, Mara's child is literally resurrected — not born but reborn.

Claudel had been stung by God's apparent rejection of him when he wanted to enter the Benedictine order, an order, moreover, whose principal object is perfection of the choral repetition of the Office. Now, with *Art poétique* and the *Odes* he discovered the role God intended for him. The poet, too, is a kind of priest, and he too celebrates the Office through his poetry. Like the architect Pierre de Craon, Claudel has much to create: "Non point les heures de l'Office dans un livre, mais les vraies, avec une cathédrale dont le soleil successif fait de toutes les parties lumière et ombre." [26] Build a cathedral, celebrate the Hour, re-create, in effect, the liturgy — it is all the same thing, a temporal imitation of the eternal.

If Claudel's metaphysical thinking is somewhat difficult to follow in the abstract, it becomes clearer in its poetic application. The *Cinq Grandes Odes* are the conscious expressions of the precepts elaborated in *Art poétique.* Claudel himself makes this unmistakenly clear in a letter to Gide in which he tells his friend:

> Ce sont de grands monologues lyriques ou je reprend poétiquement certains thèmes de mon livre de philosophie, par exemple: de l'inépuisable dans la fermeture, le cercle qui est le type de toute forme, fini et cependant infini, œuf, semence, bouche ouverte, zéro. Si Christophe Colombe était parti avec le désire de trouver un monde nouveau, ce n'au-

---

[26] *L'Annonce,* II, p. 24.

> rait été qu'un aventurier de génie. Ce qui a fait sa grandeur, c'est sa foi dans le cercle parfait. Ce que peindront mes Odes, c'est la joie d'un homme que le silence des espaces n'éffraie plus.[27]

Even the poetic techniques he used in the *Odes* grow out of his momentous attempt to "assemble reality," to repeat and imitate the eternal.

TO NAME = TO CREATE. In the first ode Claudel invokes the "presence créatrice" of the nine muses, calling each individually by name. Then he addresses himself to Mnémosyne, muse of memory, and dedicates to her these first verses. Why is Mnémosyne singled out?

> Elle est le poids spirituel. Elle est le rapport exprimé
>   par un chiffre très beau. Elle est posée d'une manière
>   qui est ineffable.
> Sur le pouls même de l'Etre.
> *Elle est l'heure intérieure*: le trésor jaillissant et la
>   source emmagasinée;
> La jointure à ce qui n'est point temps du temps exprimé
>   par le langage.[28] [italics added]

In effect, Mnémosyne represents the self-imposed task of the poet, for the poem will be the junction of what is not time with time expressed in language.

In *Traité de la Co-naissance* Claudel had written: "L'image n'est pas une portion de tout; elle en est le symbole. Elle est ce qu'il [le poète] fait; en elle comme en une monnaie marquée de la face du souverain, il rend cet être ce qu'il a reçu,"[29] and in *Les Muses*:

> Ainsi un poème n'est point comme un sac de mots, il
>   n'est point seulement
> Ces choses qu'il signifie, mais il est lui-même un signe,
>   un acte imaginaire, créant
> Le temps nécessaire à sa résolution...[30]

---

[27] *Correspondance,* Claudel, Gide, p. 91.
[28] *Les Muses,* p. 223.
[29] *Art poétique,* p. 186.
[30] *Les Muses,* p. 228.

The *Odes* actually are a gift from the poet to his Creator — "... je m'en vais faire à loisir pour vous seul un beau cantique..."[31]

In *l'Esprit et l'Eau* we find the most striking illustration of the phenomenon of co-naissance. The poet is *born with*, that is, he sees, assimilates and unifies the world around him:

> Où que je tourne la tête
> J'envisage l'immense octave de la Création!
> Le monde s'ouvre et, si large qu'en soit l'empan, mon
> regard le traverse d'un bout à l'autre. [32]

Through the word he dominates, possesses:

> Vous êtes pris et d'un bout du monde jusqu'à l'autre
> autour de Vous
> J'ai tendu l'immense rets de ma connaissance. [33]

In the "Argument" he speaks of an "Elan vers le Dieu absolu qui seul nous libère du contigent," and of a "Vision de l'éternité dans la création transitoire." For a privileged moment he is liberated from the contingent and glimpses the vision of which he had written in the conclusion of *Traité de la Co-naissance*.

> Eclate le jour nouveau, éclate dans la possession de la
> source je sais quelle jeunesse angélique!
> Mon cœur ne bat plus le temps, c'est l'instrument de
> ma perdurance,
> Et l'impérissable esprit envisage les choses passantes.
> Mais ai-je dit passantes? voici qu'elles recommencent.
> Et mortelles? il n'y a plus de mort avec moi. [34]

The poet's role is indeed a prefiguration of the role of his soul in Paradise. "Car l'image de la mort produit la mort, et l'imitation de la vie / La vie, et la vision de Dieu engendre la vie éternelle." [35]

Imitation is the key, not only to the content of the Odes, but to the verse form in which that content is expressed. Some of the procedures which Claudel uses are a direct consequence of his

---

[31] *Magnificat*, p. 250.
[32] *L'Esprit et l'Eau*, p. 240.
[33] Ibid., p. 241.
[34] Ibid.
[35] *Magnificat*, p. 253.

attempt to encompass the "ample cérémonie" of creation, and grow out of the aesthetic and metaphysical theories developed in *Art Poétique*. These are, of course, established poetic techniques; it is their use by Claudel which is extraordinary. All of them, moreover, are means of imitating.

In *Art Poétique* Claudel starts from the Aristotelian premise that the intellect draws all its natural knowledge from the senses. While it cannot then directly know the super-sensible or metaphysical, it can have indirect knowledge (Animus listens to Anima's song) by analogy. Nothing, he writes in *Connaissance du Temps*, subsists by itself, but only in relationship with all else. This is precisely how he proceeds: by analogy, or, in poetic terminology, by metaphor, re-echoing the Word which he sees and hears — for, "l'œuil écoute" — around him. In the fourth ode he writes:

> Et moi je dis qu'il n'est rien dans la nature qui soit
>   fait sans dessin et propos à l'homme adressé,
> Et comme lumière pour l'œil et le son pour l'oreille,
>   ainsi toute chose pour l'analyse de l'intelligence,
> Continuée avec l'intelligence qui la
> Refait de l'élément qu'elle récupère...[36]

It is through the metaphor that the poet can expose "la seule existence conjointe et simultanée"[37] of different things and reveal the harmony of the whole. The metaphor is the essence of newness: "...elle est l'art autochtone employé par tout ce qui naît."[38] Seldom has a poetic line been so metaphorically surcharged, or for more evident reason. As the critic Marcel Raymond observes in *De Baudelaire au Surréalisme*, "La densité métaphorique s'explique en grande partie par la volonté du poète de mettre toutes les ressources de la langue et de la poésie au service de la totale réalité qu'il a dessin d'exprimer."[39] The least complicated (the word "simple" does not apply) of his procedures is the juxtaposition of successive metaphors. Here for example, in *La Muse qui est la Grâce*, the muse speaks:

---

[36] *La Muse qui est la Grâce*, p. 267.
[37] *Art poétique*, p. 143.
[38] Ibid.
[39] Raymond Marcel, *De Baudelaire au Surréalisme* (Paris: José Corti, 1963), p. 183.

> Car je ne suis point pour toujours ici, mais je suis fragile
>   sur ce sol de la terre avec mes deux pieds qui tâtent,
> Comme un homme au fond de l'eau qui le repousse, comme un
>   oiseau qui cherche à se poser, les deux ailes à demi
>   reployées, comme la flamme sur la mèche! [40]

the poetry depending upon the cumulative effect of the metaphors.

Elsewhere he uses the same basic procedure, but expanding it and returning at length to the original comparison. In the first part of the same ode, for instance, he begins, "Et je suis comme la jeune fille à la fenêtre du chateau blanc, dans le clair de lune," a girl who hears the whistle of her lover below and the noise of the two horses he has brought for their escape, and then the metaphor changes and she becomes like a little tiger. The poet, again returning to the first person, compares himself to a winepresser as he presses his harvest of words and becomes intoxicated by the fumes. The last metaphor is in turn swallowed up by the first, and he likens the night to an illuminated ballroom where the girl attends her first dance. [41]

There are metaphors within metaphors, and words used simultaneously in their various meanings. We have seen one example in Claudel's definition of time as the *sens* of life, where he further defines *sens* to include very different connotations of that word. Take, for example, the following lines from *L'Esprit et l'Eau*.

> Vos sources ne sont point des sources. L'élément même!
> La matière première. C'est la mére, je dis, qu'il me faut!
> Possédons la mer éternelle et salée, la grande rose grise!
>   Je lève un bras vers le paradis. Je m'avance vers la mer
>   aux entrailles de raisin. [42]

Here, in the first line, we have the double meaning of *source*, as the origin and, differentiated by the partitive *des*, as a spring or source of a river. Now he plays on the words *mère* and *mer*, voluntarily confusing them because in his mind there is an identification, the eternal sea being the mother of all life, and then ... the great grey rose. Finally he completes the identification: "Je lève un bras

---

[40] *La Muse qui est la Grâce*, p. 268.
[41] Ibid., p. 264.
[42] *L'Esprit et l'Eau*, p. 236.

vers le paradis." Still the sea, but now also the sky. Here we have that circular movement. The metaphor, like an enormous flower, encompasses both sea and sky which are in turn identified with the source of all life, and which form a closed whole.

The poem is in fact an imitation of life. For if the sea represents life, the ode is likened to the sea:

Voici l'Ode, voici cette grande Ode nouvelle vous est présente,
Non point comme une chose qui commence, mais peu à peu comme
    la mer qui était là,
La mer de toutes les paroles humaines avec la surface en
    divers endroits
Reconnue par un souffle sous le brouillard et par l'œil
    de la matrone lune! [43]

What else is the *Magnificat* but a great imitation, paralleling, re-echoing the song of Mary? "Mon Dieu, qui nous parlez avec les paroles mêmes que nous vous adressons," [44] and this line has specific as well as general application, for Claudel follows to a great extent the biblical Magnificat, beginning his ode with the same words, "Mon âme magnifie le Seigneur," and ending with "Et selon la parole que Vous avez donné à nos pères, à Abraham et à sa semence dans tous les siècles. Ainsi soit-il!" traces the long road from his conversion to the writing of the ode, and gives thanks to God "Parce qu'il m'a éte fait des choses grandes et que le Saint est son nom!" (Luke I, 49). Like the Virgin, he puts himself entirely at the disposition of God, like her, praises Him for this child born to him. Even his unkind references to the Voltaires, the Renans, the Michelets and the Hugos are buttressed by biblical verse: "Parce que vous avez dispersé les orgueilleux et ils ne peuvent être ensemble." (Luke I, 51). With her he marvels that the poor and the humble are chosen, "and the rich He has sent empty away." (Luke I, 53).

It is at once the new father and the poet who speak, and it is to the *child* and the *poem* that he refers:

    La chair crée la chair, et l'homme l'enfant qui n'est pas
        pour lui, et l'esprit

---

[43] Ibid., p. 239.
[44] *Magnificat*, p. 250.

> La parole adressée à d'autres esprits.
> Comme la nourrice encombrée de son lait débordant, ainsi
>   le poète de cette parole en lui à d'autres adressée. [45]

The ode is superposed on the poet's life. He himself is now at the "post-meridian," the afternoon of life, looking forward to the promised land he longs to enter: "Restez avec moi, Seigneur, parce que le soir approche et ne m'abandonnez pas!" and "Laissez-moi envahir Votre séjour intelligible à cette heure postméridienne!" [46] The song which he sings *is* the Magnificat, as is also *the act of singing it*; that is, Claudel's life and his poem have become identified and assimilated into the hour of Vespers and the Magnificat, sung at that time.

> Ce n'est pas *l'Invitatoire de Matines,* ni le *Laudate* dans
>   l'ascension du soleil et le cantique des Enfants dans
>   la fournaise!
> Mais c'est l'heure où l'homme s'arrête et considère ce
>   qu'il a fait lui-même et son œuvre conjointe à celle
>   de la journée,
> Et tout le peuple en lui s'assemble pour le *Magnificat*
>   à l'heure de Vêpres où le soleil prend mesure de la terre..." [47]

Thus by analogy does Claudel proceed: in a sort of ever-expanding metaphor he seeks a final apotheosis which, pushing language to the limits of comprehension and sometimes beyond, causes it almost to explode. The ode ends with such an explosion. The *il* referring to himself, Claudel writes:

> Et tout à l'heure il va Vous prendre entre ses bras, comme
>   Marie vous prit entre ses bras,
> Et mêlé à ce groupe au chœur qui officie dans le soleil
>   et dans la fumée,
> Vous montrer à l'obscure génération qui arrive,
> La lumière pour la révélation des nations et le salut de
>   Votre peuple Israël... [48]

"Toute parole une répétition," Claudel wrote in *Les Muses*. His use of two techniques — enumeration and repetition — are a direct

---

[45] Ibid., p. 259.
[46] Ibid., p. 261.
[47] Ibid., p. 262.
[48] Ibid., p. 263.

consequence, as is the metaphoric surcharge, of his desire to put down the whole in its harmony. Englobing the earth, his delight is in enumerating what he sees, recreating it through the evocative magic of the word. The beginning of *l'Esprit et l'Eau* offers a fine example of the effect of this enumeration combined with repetition. The ode was written in Peking — "Or, maintenant, près d'un palais couleur de souci dans les arbres aux toits nombreux ombrageant un trône pourri / J'habite d'un vieux empire le décombre principal," [49] — where the poet keenly felt his distance from the sea. Then, in a development which is perhaps intentionally unclear, he begins to speak of the "Cité carée":

> C'est ainsi que dans le vieux vent de la Terre, la Cité
>   carée dresse ses retranchements et ses portes,
> Etage ses Portes colossales dans le vent jaune, trois fois
>   trois portes comme des éléphants,
> Dans le vent de cendre et de poussière, dans le grand vent
>   gris de la poudre qui fut Sodome, et les empires d'Egypte
>   et des Perses, et Paris, et Tadmor, et Babylone. [50]

The city described is Peking, famous for its inner walled city. In the description is an example of one type of repetition, that of the word itself, repeated and qualified: "Portes colossales," "trois fois trois portes," "vieux vent de la Terre," "vent jaune," "vent de cendre et de poussière," "grand vent gris de la poudre." Through the repetition Claudel achieves an almost suffocating atmosphere of decay and death. The poet is walled in. The dry wind that blows through Peking is composed of the dust of dead cities and pagan empires (and Paris is included in the enumeration!).

Having evoked his prison through the word, he can now break out of it:

Mais que m'importent à présent vos empires, et tout ce qui meurt,
Et vous autres que j'ai laissées, votre voie hideuse là-bas!
Puisque je suis libre! [51]

---

[49] *L'Esprit et l'Eau*, p. 235.
[50] Ibid.
[51] Ibid.

Because his place is not with those things which are created but with that which creates, he finds once more "l'esprit liquide et lascif." [52]

These continual repetitions — of sounds, words, rhythms and particularly of the initial word — have an almost hypnotic effect on the reader. It is sometimes like a litany: in only two verses in the *Magnificat*, beginning "Bénédiction sur la terre," the word *bénédiction* appears seven times! An extraordinary instance of anaphoric repetition, reminiscent of the Bible, is found in the opening lines of *L'Esprit et l'Eau*.

> Après le long silence
> Après le grand silence civil de maints jours tout fumant
>   de rumeurs et de fumées,
> Haleine de la terre en culture et ramage des grandes villes
>   dorées,
> Soudain l'Esprit de nouveau, soudain le souffle de nouveau,
> Soudain le coup sourd au cœur, soudain le mot donné, soudain
>   le souffle de l'Esprit, le rapt sec, soudain la possession
>   de l'Esprit!
> Comme quand dans le ciel plein de nuit avant que ne claque
>   le premier feu de foudre,
> Soudain le vent de Zeus dans un tourbillon plein de pailles
>   et de poussières avec la lessive de tout le village! [53]

In this passage we have examples of all types of repetition, overlaid by the double use of anaphora. The first two lines, in the minor mood, serve as a somber musical introduction. The third line, breaking the pattern with the initial *haleine* is just that: a pause, a deep breath inhaled before the rush of wind. The sustained anaphora which follows, each verse and phrases within each verse beginning with *soudain*, underscores not only the suddenness of the wind, but its great force, the alliteration of the *s* imitating the sound of rushing air. There is a metaphoric build-up of increasing strength: the spirit is a breath, a word, a flow, a wind, a tornado.

The initial repetition is often a pronoun. When the poet begins to speak of "Mnémosyne, qui ne parle jamais!" [54] for instance, almost every phrase begins with *elle*. When he wishes to emphasize

---

[52] Ibid.
[53] Ibid., p. 234.
[54] *Les Muses*, p. 222.

his own presence "Moi, l'homme," he repeats the pronoun *je*: "J'use, je suis maître / Je suis au monde, j'exerce de toutes parts ma connaissance."⁵⁵ Claudel is intentionally imitating the Old Testament — the praise of the virtuous woman, for instance (Proverbs XXXI, 12-27) where each verse begins with *she*, or the Song of Solomon, a favorite of Claudel's, the fifth chapter of which is remarkable for the anaphoric use of the pronoun *I*.

The letter-word *O* enjoys an especially privileged place in Claudel's work, and examples are too numerous to mention. His preference for this word was probably due not only to its power of invocation (cf. the mantra *Om*) but also to its shape, for, as he wrote to Gide in the letter earlier quoted, the circle is the perfect form, "finite yet infinite, egg, seed, open mouth, zero."

In all his procedures, Claudel is striving for richness and depth. The great *rassembleur*, who liked to compare himself to Columbus, gathers the forces of language, assembles, looses them, now violent, now calm again, so that the listener is alternately buffeted by the repetitions as by blasts of wind, or quieted by their steady rhythm.

The open line used in the *Odes* adds to the general impression of intensity, the length being determined by the "spiritual breath" of the poet, "... [qui] n'ouvre pas autrement que le petit oiseau son âme, / Quand prêt à chanter de tout son corps il s'emplit d'aier jusqu'à l'intérieur de tous ces os! "⁵⁶ He is, as it were, constrained to sing by the force of his inspiration.

By its freedom and power, as well as through the poet's own metaphors, Claudel's verse inevitably reminds one of wind or water — often of ocean waves. One of the most striking examples of this undulatory movement in to be found in *L'Esprit et l'Eau*.* Here is the first wave:

Ni
Le marin, ni
Le poisson qu'un autre poisson à manger
Entraîne, mais la chose même et tout le tonneau et la veine
    vive,

---

⁵⁵ *L'Esprit et l'Eau*, p. 238.
⁵⁶ *Les Muses*, p. 226.
* The passage in question begins with the word *ni*, p. 236 (Pléiade) and ends with *l'eau*, p. 238. The movement is thus sustained at some length, there being six "waves" in all.

> Et l'eau même, et l'élément même, je joue, je resplendis!
>   Je partage la liberté de la mer omniprésente!
> L'eau

the last *l'eau* (there is no period following it) marking both the ebb point and the beginning of a second wave. The lines become successively longer, then return to the short, often one-word beginning. Thus in the passage as it continues successive waves are introduced by *l'esprit, le souffle secret; quelle; moi, l'homme;* with increasing distance between each crest to a point where the waves suddenly subside and waters gently lap the shore with the one word, *l'eau*. This movement is, in fact, so clear it could be represented diagrammatically, as below:

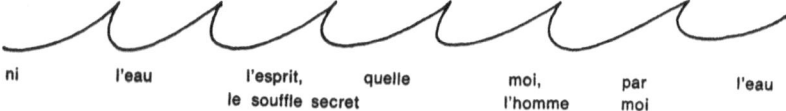

There is a final method of imitation which Claudel utilizes, though it may seem unusual to class it as such, and that is vocabulary. In an effort to imitate the kaleidoscopic variety of life, Claudel "mines" the wealth of language. Probably no French poet since Hugo has summoned to his command such a vocabulary. Nothing is beyond his reach. Colloquialisms, even dialect abound (see, for example, the workers' conversation in Act III, scene i of *L'Annonce faite à Marie*). In direct contradiction to a classicist like Valéry, he likes technical vocabulary, often employing terms associated with agriculture, the sea, even wine-making. Exotic names — Koubar, le Gange, l'Orénoque — are used for their evocative value. There are religious and mythological allusions, often obscure to the reader. Like Rabelais he coins his own words from Latin and Greek, which may appear in the original, or changed to conform to the line or his fancy (*décumane*: the tenth and largest wave). Occasionally one finds words that seem entirely of his onomatopeic invention, like *biquante,* followed by a [sic] or humbly footnoted, "Ce mot ne semble pas figurer dans les dictionnaires." He apparently assumes the reader is conversant with English, German, even Chinese!

This examination of Claudel's verse is by no means intended to be complete, but only to point up how the most striking aspects of it — the metaphoric density, the delight in enumeration and repetition, the movement, the open line, the enormous arsenal of vocabulary — all are outward signs of an inner vision, and an attempt to know, unify, and imitate Creation in its totality.

Les Cinq Grandes Odes thus form an artistic whole, the poetic translation, both in form and substance, of *Art poétique*. More than that, they are also a sort of diary of a soul. It is significant that Claudel dedicates the first lines of *Les Muses* to Mnénomyne, muse of memory, for the *Odes,* written over a period of eight years, reflect the trials and experiences through which he has passed. In the first poem he has discovered his gift as a namer and creator, and outlines his undertaking. In *L'Esprit et l'Eau* the very important theme of thirst emerges (this theme is examined in depth in Chapter IV). It is a spiritual thirst, "Mon Dieu, ayez pitié de ces eaux désirantes! / Mon Dieu, vous voyez que je ne suis pas seulement esprit, mais eau! ayez pitié de ces eaux en moi qui meurent de soif!" [57] but also a carnal thirst from which he suffers: "J'ai possédé l'interdiction. J'ai connu cette source de soif!" [58] Yet the poem ends on a note of victory, for Claudel sees before him "la Sagesse de Dieu," and the closing lines are those of the resurrected Christ, "Ne me touchez point!"

The *Magnificat* is Claudel's own song of praise and thanksgiving on the birth of his child, as it is also a stock-taking of himself in the afternoon of his life. But although he indicated submission in that ode — "Et je fus devant vous comme un lutteur qui plie / Non qu'il se croie faible, mais parce que l'autre est plus fort" [59] the spiritual struggle was not over. In *La Muse qui est la Grâce* the poet rebuffs the importunate muse, stopping his ears and recalling his deep and frustrated love, the scars of which remain unhealed: "Qui a aimé l'âme humaine, qui une fois a été compact avec l'autre âme vivante, il y reste pris pour toujours." [60]

---

[57] *L'Esprit et l'Eau*, p. 244.
[58] Ibid., p. 245.
[59] *Magnificat*, p. 249.
[60] *La Muse qui est la Grâce*, p. 276.

It is only in *La Maison fermé* that this inner struggle is ultimately resolved. If in the first ode he invoked the classical muses only to discover in the fourth that his muse *was,* in fact, Grace, in the last he turns from pagan allusion to salute the four Christian virtues of St. Thomas: Prudence, Force, Temperance, and Justice. His marriage of two years has brought him a new serenity; he has found in his wife not only a companion but a "guardian."

> Je sais que je suis ici avec Dieu et chaque matin je rouvre
>   mes yeux dans le paradis.
> Jadis j'ai connu la passion, mais maintenant je n'ai plus
>   que celle de la patience et du désir,
> De connaître Dieu dans sa fixité et d'acquérir la verité
>   par l'attention et chaque chose qui est toutes les autres
>   en la récréant avec son nom intelligible dans ma pensée.[61]

Once again he goes back in memory to his Christmas conversion, to that moment when "la foie seule était en moi," and recalls the long road he has since traveled, asking, "Et maintenant où sont ces Puissants qui nous écrasaient? il n'y a plus que quelques masques obscènes à mes pieds."[62]

He has accomplished his self-imposed task to assimilate the world and reveal its unity:

> Nous avons conquis le monde et nous avons trouvé que Votre
>   Création est finie,
> Et que l'imparfait n'a point de place avec Vos œuvres
>   finies, et que notre imagination ne peut pas ajouter
> Un seul chiffre à ce Nombre en extase devant Votre Unité![63]

The poet is the veritable possessor of the universe; he holds the stars in his fingertips: "O certitude et immensité de mon domaine! ô cher univers entre mes mains connaissantes!"[64] or again, "Tout est à moi, catholique!"[65]

Striding through this great totality Claudel sows the word, like a seed on good ground, in the hearts of men:

---

[61] *La Maison fermée,* p. 280.
[62] Ibid., p. 284.
[63] Ibid., p. 289.
[64] Ibid., p. 281.
[65] Ibid., p. 289.

> Comment Dieu entrera-t-il dans ton cœur s'il n'y a point de place,
> Si tu ne lui fais une habitation? Point de Dieu pour toi sans une église et toute vie commence par la cellule.[66]

Silently the tiny cell will grow — "...le réduit où nous recevons le Seigneur croît plus silencieusement en nous que le temple de Salomon qui fut construit sans aucun bruit de la hache et du marteau."[67]

Like Pierre de Craon, he becomes a sower of churches, where the Hours will shine through the stained glass of his poetry. Recalling the intense disappointment of Solesmes et Liguge, he now feels only exultation: "Pour la clôture de Solesmes et de Liguge voici une autre clôture! / Je vois devant moi l'Eglise catholique qui est tout l'univers!"[68] These are the words of a man who could write to his friend, "Ce que peindront mes Odes, c'est la joie d'un homme que le silence des espaces n'effraie plus."

---

[66] Ibid., p. 283.
[67] Ibid., p. 284.
[68] Ibid., p. 289.

Chapter III

...AND TIME AGAIN

> Et l'éternité même est dans le temporel
> Et l'arbre de la grâce est raciné profond
> Et plonge dans le sol et touche jusqu'au fond
> Et le temps est lui-même un temps intemporel
> *Eve*

The idea of continuous renewal is central in Claudel's concept of time: it is the sum and substance of the *Traité de la Co-naissance*. Certainly one of the reasons why he so vehemently rejected Taine and his sociological determinism was that it precluded the *new*.

It is precisely on this point that Péguy and Claudel share a common concern. Although Péguy states it in quite different terms, he, too, rejects this determinism, or what he calls, in an even more comprehensive term, *le tout fait*. Where Claudel's mentor was St. Thomas Aquinas, Péguy's was a contemporary and one of his own professors, Henri Bergson.

Bergson's influence on Péguy would be difficult to exaggerate, and the latter's admiration for his master continued undiminished all his life. Only a few months before his death he wrote, referring to himself in the third person: "L'autre est, après Bergson, et j'oserais presque dire avec Bergson, le seul bergsonien qui sache de quoi on parle. Il a été l'élève de Bergson à l'Ecole normale. Il a gardé pour Bergson une fidélité filiale." [1] When Bergson's work was menaced with inclusion on the Index, Péguy came to the defense of the philosopher in two long articles, "Note sur M. Bergson et la Philo-

---
[1] "Note conjointe sur M. Descartes," II, p. 1362.

sophie bergsonienne" (in which he writes at greater length on Descartes) and the unfinished "Note conjointe sur M. Descartes et la Philosophie cartésienne" (in which, conversely, he concentrates on Bergson).

All the good images have already been used by Péguy's biographers — Roger Secrétain (Péguy, *Soldat de la Verité*) compares Bergson to a sort of Lohengrin coming to the rescue of the world, Marjorie Villiers, *Péguy: A Study in Integrity,* to Sainte George slaying the deterministic dragon. Such metaphors would have pleased Péguy, who saw in Bergson a knight errant whose attack on modern thought was a maneuver worthy of Napoleon. In one fell blow, Bergson had destroyed the detested *tout fait.* In fact, Bergson triggered an explosion within Péguy comparable to Claudel's religious illumination, and paved the way for Péguy's return to faith. As we shall see, Péguy would take Bergson's theory of the *durée réelle* even farther than the philosopher himself, applying it to all areas of life. After his disciple's death Bergson acknowledged: "Beaucoup de personnes m'ont fait l'honneur d'écrire sur moi. Personne, en dehors des éloges immérites qu'il m'a donnés, ne l'a fait comme Péguy. Il avait un don merveilleux pour franchir la matérialité des êtres, la dépasser et pénétrer jusqu'à leur âme. C'est ainsi qu'il a connu ma pensée la plus sécrète, telle que je ne l'ai pas exprimée, telle que j'aurais voulu l'exprimer." [2]

Just how was this liberation effected? According to Bergson, exact science depends upon a spatial and quantitative concept of time. We assume that each moment of a given length is "equal" to every other moment of that length, like metric divisions on a ruler. Thus, if the speed and trajectory of a comet is known it is possible to postulate with utmost accuracy its position at a given time in the future or past. Now, while this sort of linear time is useful in the exact sciences, it is misleading when applied to the *organic,* * and specifically, to human behavior. Everyone knows that moments of time are not equal, that a minute of pain in a dentist's chair may seem far longer than a pleasant hour spent listening to a concert. The difference is not in quantity but in quality, and can-

---

[2] Tharaud, II, p. 222.

* Péguy gives a rather peculiar meaning to this word. By the organic he means that which follows the plan of nature, and is consequently vital, healthy, alive.

not therefore be measured quantitatively. It can, however, be seized upon by the intuition. To use a Bergsonian metaphor, a moment is like one note in a melody. We may identify this note as *E flat,* but it will be like no other E flat because it will be affected by the notes which precede and follow it. Marcel Proust, himself a student of Bergson, affords an excellent example of the application of this theory in *A la Recherche du Temps perdu.* Each time Swann listens to the Vinteuil sonata, and specifically, to *la petite phrase,* his inner experience varies. The first time he hears it the mysterious pleasure that the tittle phrase evokes almost eludes him. It is only afterwards, through memory, that he is able to reconstruct the phrase and savor its delicacies. Later these measures will come to represent his love for Odette. But, although the same notes are played in the same amount of time, their qualitative effect on Swann is never identical, that effect being far more dependent on the stage to which Swann and Odette have progressed in their love affair than on the music itself. Others in the audience cannot duplicate Swann's experience, although they share the same moment, because they do not share Swann's associations. These memories and associations constitute for Swann *la durée réelle.*

At the same time as Bergson destroyed the *tout fait* he restored, through his concept of interpenetration of moments, the variety and multiplicity of the organic:

> Distinguons donc, pour conclure, deux formes de la multiplicité, deux appréciations bien différentes de la vie consciente. Au-dessous de la durée homogène, symbole extensif de la durée vraie dont les moments hétérogènes se pénètrent; au-dessous de la multiplicité numérique des états conscients, une multiplicité qualitative; au-dessous du moi aux états bien définis, un moi où succession implique fusion et organisation.[3]

How delighted Péguy was to have this precious multiplicity restored! And not just the variations between individuals, but those within a single person. This pluralism, which is the heart of human liberty, Péguy had stressed in his "Harmonious City," where every citizen was free to follow ... and, if he wished, to change ... his

---

[3] Henri Bergson, *Essai sur les données immédiates de la conscience* (Paris: Félex Alcan, 1936), p. 97.

natural inclinations. In fact, in his early writings, Péguy had criticized Christianity because it would reduce the multiplicity to unity.

Herein lies one of the dilemmas of the modern world which he examines at great length in his remarkable essay, "Clio, Dialogue de l'Histoire et de l'Ame païenne." Clio, muse of history, complains of the impossibility of her task. How is she to capture the multiplicity of reality! She cannot even exhaust the present, much less document the past. Modern civilization, says Clio, operates on a false *caisse d'épargne* or savings bank premise. People act as if they could quietly catalogue facts, put them into a sort of savings bank of documents, where they would be permanently stored, the balance of which account would continually accrue. Poor Clio! How can she explain one event without going back to the events that led to it, and then to those which led to these, and so on? And how can she begin to be sure that she had taken everything into consideration? If she attempts to explain antiquity, she lacks documents. If she turns her attention to the contemporary world instead, she is inundated with them, a large portion false, misleading, contradictory. Clio complains that she has been given a job as hopeless as that of pursuing an auto on foot.

Because many of the supposed "facts" are not that at all, they falsify reality. True history (which Péguy calls "chronicles" to make a distinction) must thus be written *contre les documents*. If Clio were permitted to seize the salient facts intuitively, what a history she would write! "moi aussi je saurais voir un mot sur une cime, et les éclairements profonds d'une situation."[4] But this intuitive approach is exactly what has been proscribed by modern historians and sociologists: "Qu'une ligne, qu'un mot éclaire un monde, cela, c'est un procédé d'art, permettez-moi de vous le dire, et les procédés d'art dans le monde moderne sont précisément tout ce qui demeure interdit."[5]

The importance of this intuitive approach in Péguy's work is obvious. Like Michelet or Joinville, whom he admiringly refers to as "chroniclers," Péguy would attempt to "resurrect" the past. When he wrote his first *Jeanne d'Arc* he had approached the subject as a historian, even though, as we have seen, he was already

---

[4] "Clio," II, p. 247.
[5] Ibid., p. 246.

haunted by Jeanne's "inner life." *Le Mystère de la Charité,* composed after Bergson's impact had been assimilated, is exclusively concerned with this inner or real life, as are all his successive poetic works.

There are also stylistic implications, particularly in his prose writing. One of the most disconcerting aspects of Péguy's essays is the apparent lack of organization. "Clio" is a case in point. It begins with a discussion of how one should read a book, goes from there to Greek mythology, Antigone, and then abruptly, to *Les Châtiments* of Hugo, *Tartuffe, Le Mariage de Figaro,* without warning to the problems of writing history, Bergson, and so on, doubling back again and again to Hugo, or Greek tragedy or the Olympian gods. All these digressions, which seem tangential, are really not so. The same can be said of the apparent "repetitions" with which both his prose and poetry are encumbered. As Gide very acutely observed:

> Le style de Péguy est semblable aux cailloux du desert, qui se suivent et se ressemblent, où chacun est pareil à l'autre, mais un tout petit peu différent; d'une différence qui se reprend, se ressaisit, se répète, semble se répéter, s'accentue, s'affirme, et toujours plus nettement; on avance! Qu'ai-je à faire de plus de variété! [6]

In both digressions and repetitions, Péguy is illustrating his own theory: he is trying to convey the multiplicity, the infinite shadings of the particular reality he would evoke for the reader.

Les modernes (one of several contemptuous labels) reject such an intuitive approach because dimly, half-consciously, they suspect it will prove uncomfortable. The moment the multiplicity of the reality is experienced, man is overwhelmed; he is once more reminded of the transitory, fragile nature of his own condition.

It is this experience of the *present* that he wishes at all cost to avoid, and which, through an historical or "scientific" approach he can indeed manage to avoid:

> Sous prétexte que la *date* du présent sera, deviendra dans un certain futur une *date* du passé, sous prétexte que la

---

[6] André Gide, "Journal sans dates," NRF, III, 1 (March 1910), p. 403.

> date d'aujourd'hui sera demain la date d'hier on croyait que le présent lui-même, que l'être du présent, était ce qui dans un certain futur sera un certain passé. Et que cette notion épuisait le présent, l'être même du présent, qu'elle nous en donnait une connaissance intégrale et absolue. Et que, par conséquent, (puisque c'était le même être), que ce n'était pas la peine de se donner tant de mal pour connaître le présent, puisqu'on allait le connaître si facilement dans un instant, tout de suite, aussitôt qu'il serait passé.[7]

Since any attempt to know, that is, to *live* the present is fraught with such difficulty and discomfort, let us wait a moment, the present will become the past and therefore classifiable. Péguy, putting words into the mouth of *les modernes,* humorously sums up their attitude: "*Aujourd'hui,* pensait-on, est un mauvais garçon; et un garçon; et un garçon mal élevé. Et puis on ne sait pas bien qui il est. Il nous ferait des ennuis. Attendons seulement un jour. Dès demain il sera hier. Et nous le retrouverons dans le compartiment des hiers à la Bibliothèque Nationale."[8]

The error in this thinking is that of equating the *date* (again, a number or "document") with the *essence* of the present. If we wait a moment, it is just that moment which changes the present in its essence. Péguy insists

> ...qu'il y a dans le présent un certain être propre. Et qu'attendre pour le mieux connaître, c'est déjà lui faire subir la seule altération qui compte... qu'aujourd'hui est aujourd'hui, un certain être propre, et non pas seulement, et même en un certain sens, non pas du tout ce qui demain sera hier.
>
> Que le présent est le présent. Qu'il n'est pas un futur antérieur, un moyen terme entre le futur et le passé, entre l'ultérieur et l'antérieur.[9]

By a very different route Péguy has here come close to Claudel's idea of an absolute or eternal present.

Now the link between this Bergsonian concept of the present and Christian faith becomes clear:

---

[7] "Note conjointe sur M. Descartes," II, p. 1513.
[8] Ibid., p. 1514.
[9] Ibid., p. 1516.

> ... quand il nous réinstalle dans cette situation, dans cette position du présent M. Bergson en cela même et déjà par cela seul nous réintroduit dans une situation et dans une position chrétienne, dans la seule situation et dans la seule position chrétienne, il nous fait littéralement retrouver le point de chrétienté, le point de vue, le point de vie et le point d'être de chrétienté. Car il nous remet dans le précaire, et dans le transitoire, et dans ce dévêtu qui fait proprement la condition de l'homme.[10]

There is an interesting comparison here. Both Claudel and Péguy are intent upon experiencing to the fullest extent this present. Even their terminology is similar: Claudel speaks of "possessing" the present, Péguy uses the verb *to seize*: "... saisir le présent dans le présent même." It is in their methods of attaining possession that the two poets differ radically. Claudel developed the Rimbaldean mystique of the word within a Christian context: the poet "creates," "possesses" life through imitation. Eventually there is a superposition of the *word* on the *Word*. Such metaphysical conjecturing would have seemed to Péguy — had he thought of it at all — as dangerous intellectualizing. Ignoring intellectual means, Péguy would choose the path of *intuition* and *memory*.

It is often necessary to clarify Péguy's peculiar use of words. When he writes that through memory we can seize the present, he is not using this term in its general sense. In fact, he opposes the two words, *souvenir* and *mémoire*. Clio makes the distinction. Ask an old man about some event of his youth: "Alors au lieu de s'enfoncer dans sa mémoire, *il fait appel à ses souvenirs*. A une remémoration organique il préfère un retracé historique... l'homme, dit-elle, aimera toujours mieux se mesurer que de se voir."[11] Earlier I had used the example of Swann. When Swann, through memory, evokes not just the notes (which would have been a "*retracé historique*") but all the subtle sensations, emotions and associations Vinteuil's phrase had caused in him, he is making a "*remémoration*" such as Clio describes. Contemporary history, Clio continues, is nothing but indexed "souvenirs," whereas memory is the key to truth. "Regardez dans votre mémoire et ainsi et en elle dans la mémoire de votre peuple. Regardez comme il faut regarder dans

---

[10] Ibid., p. 1520.
[11] "Clio," II, p. 286.

cet ordre de regard, sans arrière pensée, comme c'est, sans souci de calcul et de raisonnement," [12] Clio counsels. And if he follows her instructions, the poet will make a momentous discovery. At this point Clio (Péguy) seems to go beyond Bergson, for if one does go back beyond his personal memory into a sort of collective, racial memory, he will discover that the qualitative *durée* which Bergson showed exists for the individual also exists for institutions, movements, peoples, nations. "Il est indéniable que tout le temps ne passe pas avec la même vitesse et selon le même rythme," Clio begins, and then continues:

> Non pas seulement le temps individuel, non pas seulement ce temps personnel. Cela c'est entendu depuis Bergson ... Mais le temps public même, le temps de tout un peuple, le temps du monde, on est conduit à se demander si le temps public même ne recouvre pas seulement ... une durée publique elle-même, une durée d'un peuple, une durée du monde. Et voilà ce qui ferait une sociologie, si ces gens-là étaient capables de trouver le point d'intéressement. [13]

And herein lies a concept of the greatest importance in Péguy's time system, the very complex, sometimes contradictory idea of *vieillissement*, which operates within individuals and civilizations, in fact, in all forms of organic life.

Péguy rejected the "savings bank" approach to life, because he thought it "inorganic." Nature does not work this way. In all living things there is a continual using up or fretting away, and this process is ineluctable. To seize the present in its infinite variety, the individual must make a sort of return within and upon himself by means of memory. But this action is, in essence, a process of *vieillissement*. "Le vieillissement est essentiellement ... une opération de retour, et de regret. De retour en soi-même, sur soi-même, sur son âge, ou plûtot sur l'âge antécédent en ce qu'il devient son âge, l'âge actuel ... Le vieillissement est essentiellement une opération de mémoire ... Or c'est la mémoire qui fait toute la profondeur de l'homme." [14]

---

[12] Ibid., p. 299.
[13] Ibid.
[14] Ibid., p. 270.

"Clio," it should be noted here, was written during a very difficult period for Péguy. In fact, it ends on a sad and prophetic note. Clio tells Péguy he will never reach even his fiftieth birthday. He cannot imagine himself presiding over the fiftieth series of the *Cahiers*. "Mais vous vous représentez fort bien, et je me représente avec vous (mon enfant, me dit-elle avec une grande douceur), ce que vous penserez le jour de votre mort." [15] His marriage had deteriorated, and to friends he wrote that he felt himself a stranger in his own home. The Baudoins, who had never really accepted him, were outraged by his conversion. For their sake he did not formalize it, and so both he and his children technically remained outside the Church, a situation which caused him much anguish. By his personal intransigence and bitter attacks on former friends (Jaurès, Herr, etc.) he had alienated most of them and isolated himself. He was also deeply (and hopelessly) in love with another woman (v. Chap. V). The precarious financial state of his *Cahiers* necessitated miracles of economy and energy which had worn Péguy out prematurely. In Claudel's *Magnificat,* written in the corresponding period of that poet's life, one hears the voice of a man who suddenly realizes that youth is behind him, age and death await ("Restez avec moi, Seigneur, parce que le soir approche..."). So it is, too, with Péguy, and surely his age and life's disappointments explain part of his insistence on this process of aging, which is described as at once a sad and beautiful thing. If, as he says, again is essentially an operation of regret, still, "... rien n'est aussi grand et aussi beau que le regret; ... les plus beaux poèmes sont des poèmes de regret." [16]

There are no exceptions: everyone must grow old, but there is a vast difference in the manner of aging. Péguy compares Leconte de Lisle, who simply ages and becomes *vieux* with Victor Hugo, who grows older and becomes *un vieillard*. It is Hugo's vibrant interest in the world around him and his energetic participation that makes the difference. He moved with his century. "Vieillir ce n'est pas *avoir changé* d'âge; c'est changer d'âge ou plûtot c'est avoir trop persérvéré dans le même âge." [17] There is, then, a need

---

[15] Ibid., p. 308.
[16] Ibid., p. 270.
[17] Ibid., p. 268.

for continual renewal within the individual of which he (even Hugo) must eventually become incapable.

The concept of *vieillissement* is further developed in the "Note Conjointe" in a remarkably existentialist manner. Death (and spiritual may precede physical death) occurs at that point when the soul is so saturated with memory (i.e., with living) that there is no more room. It then moves into history. This inevitable "victory" of history over the individual finds a striking parallel in Sartre. Man creates his essence by acting, and through his actions, changes constantly. Death ends the possibility of both action and change. The person once more becomes an "object" at the mercy of the living. This is Garcin's dilemma in Sartre's *Huis Clos,* and what the former means by the comment, "Je suis tombé dans le domaine public." Péguy, like Sartre, stresses the need to be able to change and create oneself:

> Une âme morte est une âme toute entière envahie de *tout fait,* toute entière occupée, toute entière consacrée au tout fait ... pleine de residus, pleine de son débris; pleine de son habitude et pleine de sa mémoire. C'est une âme qui n'a plus un atome de place, et plus un atome de matière spirituelle, pour du *se faisant.* Pour faire du se faisant.[18]

When this occurs before physical death, then, says Péguy, the person ceases to live and merely survives: *vivre* vs. *survivre.*

What is true for an individual is also true for civilizations, Clio has said. Because of the interpenetration of moments there are no abrupt breaks, yet civilizations gradually lose their youth and vigor, age and at last disappear. In Péguy's view, history must not be a superficial, or horizontal glancing-over, but rather an excavation process. He compares succeeding ages to a city, the latest buildings of which hide the cities beneath. Each succeeding city depends, then, for its foundation, on the city which preceded it. "C'est de la cité païenne que fut faite la cité chrétienne, c'est de la cité antique que fut faite la cité de Dieu, et non pas, et nullement d'un zéro de cité."[19] For him, there were two antiquities: the Greek (or

---

[18] "Note conjointe sur M. Descartes," II, p. 1403.
[19] "Clio," II, p. 252.

Greco-Roman) and the Hebrew, and without these the Christian city would not even exist.

The pagan city, moreover, was not without its own purity and piety. Says Clio, "Rien n'était aussi pur que la cité antique et le foyer antique et je dirai rien n'était aussi pieux et je dirai rien n'était aussi sacré."[20] How does Péguy, the Christian, explain this curious statement, when even the Church, to avoid damning the ancients, could think of nothing better than consigning them to Limbo? Péguy speaks of a secret, anterior grace enjoyed by antiquity, and goes on to question whether the official religion of the Olympian gods was not, perhaps, only the apparent religion, "la religion de surface et de couverture," and further, "si la profonde et si la réelle religion antique ne fut point la religion des hôtes, la religion de la supplication antique."[21] It is, incidentally, most typical of Péguy to discover some way of arranging for the salvation of the ancients, and just one more example of what Rolland called "cette révolte irrépressible contre l'Enfer et contre l'idée de damnation... qui semblait faire partie du plus profond de sa nature!"[22]

The purity which he attributed to antiquity is essentially a *sense of the tragic* and it is intimately linked with his idea of *vieillissement*.* Now, according to Clio, the reason that the Olympian gods are themselves indefensible, while Greek civilization *is* defensible, is that the gods *could not grow old and could not die*. The heroes in Greek literature, not the gods, are great. Read Homer carefully, says Péguy. "Il est impossible de ne pas être frappé d'un certain mépris très particulier qu'il y a pour les dieux."[23] And then he develops this point at great length.

> Mépris de quoi? Mépris au fond de ce que les dieux ne sont point périssables et qu'ainsi ils ne sont point revêtus

---

[20] Ibid.
[21] Ibid., p. 253.
[22] Romain Rolland, *Péguy*, II (Paris: A. Michel, 1944), p. 208.

* Once, while at Sainte-Barbe, Péguy had won what he called "la bataille d'Orange" with his mother, getting her permission and the necessary money for a ten-day trip to Orange to see Mounet Sully play Oedipus and Julie Bardet, Antigone, in the Roman amphitheater there. This visual introduction to Greek tragedy made a profound impression on him, and many pages of Clio are devoted to the character of Antigone.

[23] "Clio," II, p. 257.

> de la plus grande, de la plus poignante grandeur. Qui est précisément d'être périssables.
>
> ...Mépris précisément de ce qu'ils demeurent et de ce qu'ils ne passent point. Mépris de ce qu'ils recommencent tout le temps et non point comme l'homme, qui ne passe qu'une fois. Mépris de ce qu'ils ne sont point comme l'homme, profondément, essentiellement irréversible. Mépris de ce qu'ils ne sont point précaires, et temporaires.
>
> Mépris de ce qu'ils n'ont la triple grandeur de l'homme, la mort, la misère, le risque...[24]

For, says Péguy, Christianity did not invent *de nihilo* what he calls *les trois misères* (les trois grandeurs). The gods, then, cannot be as great as Oedipus, for he, having left the summit, made the greatest spiritual descent possible, "par le plus âpre des chemins" became "le plus misérable, le plus errant des aveugles."[25] They cannot equal Antigone because she can risk and sacrifice her life. In Homer, in Greek tragedy, risk and suffering are man's lot, death the fulfillment of his destiny.

By an extraordinarily circuitous route Péguy thus arrives at an idea central to his entire philosophic and religious system (and which finds a parallel in Claudel's works). Death, of a man or of a civilization, is the ultimate fulfillment because without it there can be no regeneration.

> Le cèdre le plus immense ne peut donner un autre cèdre, un cèdre encore plus immense, il ne peut donner son immense héritier qu'en passant par un certain point d'être et de race qui est non pas même le fruit du cèdre mais le germe qui est dans le fruit.[26]

This was the role of the Hebrews:

> Ainsi cette immense mystique d'Israël avait couvert tout un peuple et cette immense et universelle mystique de Jésus devait couvrir le monde. Mais l'une ne pouvait donner l'autre qu'en passant par un certain point d'être et de génération spirituelle.[27]

---

[24] Ibid., pp. 258-259.
[25] Ibid., p. 260.
[26] "Note conjointe sur M. Descartes," II, p. 1483.
[27] Ibid.

Ultimately Jesus, too, could fulfill his destiny only in the act of dying. People talk too much about an "imitation of Christ," says Péguy, who wonders at Jesus' perfect imitation of man, even to death.

There is nothing particularly new or remarkable in this concept, to which Péguy arrived in such a laborious fashion. But it is precisely his method of arrival and his use of the concept which are original.

At this point I must seem to digress, even as Péguy himself does to explore his subtleties. He tells the story of Courbet, the painter, talking to a young man, also an artist, who had come to see the master. When he asked without interest and through mere politeness, what might be the young man's plans, the latter replied, "I am going to the Orient." Immediately Courbet was all attention: **"vous n'avez donc pas de pays!"** he replied (as indicated, this reply is reproduced in boldface, very rare in Péguy's printed works). Péguy explains. Just as there are geographic countries, there are historic countries, zones and climates. When he himself hears of some young person leaving for an archeological voyage to distant lands, he, too, thinks, "Vous n'avez donc pas de pays."

> C'est à dire vous n'avez donc pas un endroit dans le temps (*de quel endroit que tu es, disaient les anciens aux conscrits*). Un lieu dans le temps pour ainsi dire, un temps où vous soyez homme, citoyen, soldat, père, électeur, contribuable, auteur, toutes les inévitables, toutes les irréparables, toutes les sacrées sottises.[28]

And, he continues, Homer, Plato, Corneille, Rembrandt, all had local, temporal countries. Then he adds, parenthetically and almost as an afterthought, the essence of his argument:

> (Jésus avait un pays. Et il n'est point venu sur toute la terre au hasard, mais il est venu sur toute la terre partant de la Judée; et il n'est point venu dans tout le temps et dans l'éternité au hasard, mais il est venu dans tout le temps et dans l'éternité partant d'un certain point du temps.)[29]

---

[28] "Clio," II, p. 265.
[29] Ibid., p. 266.

This, then, is the fundamental error "historians" have made. Pretending to be of two eras at once — their own and that of which they write — they undertake the impossible, for only the gods could perform such a feat.* As a result, they can only make of Jesus an *historical* subject, divorcing him from his time and place, that is, from his own *present*. Péguy makes his point perfectly clear in "Clio"!

> La plus grande disgrâce qui pourrait arriver au monde... c'est, ce serait que le monde fut admis à se faire *historien* de l'affaire Jésus;... que Jésus devint matière d'histoire et d'inscription; (au lieu d'être ce qu'il est essentiellement, matière de mémoire, matière de vieillissement et *par suite* et seulement par suite source d'un rejeunissement éternel); [30]

In short, *it is only through the mediation of the present that the eternal can be attained.* Péguy elaborates his conclusion even more precisely in the "Note conjointe sur M. Descartes." Here he states that only by living in and through the present — one's own present — can one obtain grace, understanding, salvation. The triumph of Jesus over Moses, of the new law over the old, of grace over nature and the Gospels over the prophecies is only intelligible "pour celui qui a considéré la singulière advenue, l'évènement, la survenue du futur sur le passé par le ministère du présent." [31]

Péguy's logic at this point is very simple to follow, and it is here that he owes his greatest debt to Bergson — *car il nous remet dans le précaire.* Once man opens himself to the inexhaustible multiplicity of the present he becomes conscious of his frailty, his vulnerability, his tiny place in the immensity surrounding him. Only at that moment is he open to God's grace. That opening, which he compares to a wound, is the sudden knowledge of sin, weakness, imperfection in one's self and the temporal world, the realization of human insufficiency. A most necessary wound, this, for "La charité même de Dieu ne panse point celui qui n'a pas des plaies." [32]

---

* This idea, too, is similar to Sartre's. Roquentin, in *La Nausée,* eventually discovers he cannot be of two eras at the same time.

[30] Ibid., p. 293.
[31] "Note conjointe sur M. Descartes," II, p. 1485.
[32] Ibid., p. 1390.

As Péguy describes this psychic phenomenon one is reminded of the existentialist *prise de conscience* of absurdity and anguish. There is the same dynamic aspect: "Le présent se fait tandis que le passé est *tout fait* comme aussi le futur, puisqu'il est 'du passé pour plus tard.' "[33] He realizes and accepts the fact that men are not happy. "... il sait le grand secret, de toute créature... Il sait; et il sait qu'il sait. Il sait que *l'on* n'est pas heureux. Il sait que depuis qu'il y a l'homme nul homme jamais n'a été heureux."[34]

It is this secret that the *historien*, the *honnête homme* (in short) *l'homme moderne* wishes to deny at all costs. Refusing to live in reality, he takes refuge in his "facts." His soul, says Péguy, is sealed as if with varnish. "Les 'honnêtes gens' ne mouillent pas à la grâce."[35] This image, interestingly, is very close to one Sartre uses in *Reflections sur la question juive*: those of bad faith do not wish to be *ouvert*. They choose *l'imperméabilité*.

There is also a parallel to existential liberty. Situated in the present — *le se faisant* — man is not predetermined but free. He is free to accept or to reject God's grace. But where existential liberty is awesome because it makes man totally responsible for himself and his values, Péguy's liberty gives man the terrible opportunity of failing God. In *Le Porche de la Deuxième Vertu* he writes:

Nous pouvons lui manquer.
Ne pas répondre à son appel.
Ne pas répondre à son espérance. Faire défaut. Manquer.
   Ne pas être là.
Effrayant pouvoir.
Les calculs de Dieu par nous peuvent ne pas tomber juste.
Les prévisions, les prévoyances, les providences de Dieu
Par nous peuvent ne pas tomber juste,
Par la faute de l'homme pécheur.
Les conseils de Dieu par nous peuvent manquer.
La sagesse de Dieu par nous peut défaillir.
Effrayante liberté de l'homme.[36]

He never tires of wondering at this strange paradox:

---

[33] "Note sur M. Bergson et la Philosophie bergsonienne," II, p. 1324.
[34] "Clio," II, p. 299.
[35] "Note conjointe sur M. Descartes," II, p. 1390.
[36] *Le Porche de la Deuxième Vertu*, p. 616.

> Comme Jésus dans les siécles des siécles a remis son corps
> Dans les pauvres églises
> A la discrétion du dernier des soldats,
> Ainsi Dieu dans les siécles a remis son espérance
> A la discrétion du derniers des pécheurs.
> Comme la victime se rend aux mains du bourreau,
> Ainsi Jésus s'est livré en nos mains.[37]

And he repeats, like a child in awe: "Dieu a *besoin* de nous, Dieu a *besoin* de sa créature."

In the Introduction I mentioned that whereas Claudel sometimes assumes gigantic proportions, Péguy "makes himself small." In *La Maison fermée* Claudel becomes the veritable possessor of the universe, through his participation in God: "O certitude et immensité de mon domaine! O cher univers entre mes mains connaissantes!" he can cry. Put another way, Claudel deals from a position of strength. But Péguy, from a position of weakness and vulnerability — precisely because of that vulnerability — achieves the same end. The temporal becomes a necessary adjunct to the eternal. In a sense, it holds the eternal in its power: "Le Créateur a besoin de sa créature. Il ne peut rien faire sans elle."[38]

At the very heart of this idea of a superposition of the temporal on the eternal is the incarnation of Jesus. In *Eve,* Jesus' first words to Eve are "O mère..." by which he acknowledged the human part of his nature. Péguy (referring to himself in the third person) explained in a critical article what the poet was doing.

> En revêtant cette forme d'une longue invocation de Jésus à Eve, Péguy se plaçait d'emblée et pour ainsi dire géométriquement à la croisée, au point de croisement et de recoupement des plus grands mystères de la foi... Il se plaçait résolument en ce point central, doublement axial, par où tout passe. Il se plaçait instantanément dans l'axe du spirituel et dans l'axe du charnel, dans l'axe du temporel et dans l'axe de l'éternel. Il se donnait ensemble le maximum d'homme et pour ainsi dire le maximum de Dieu. *Et Verbum caro factum est,* c'est-à-dire qu'il se plaçait au cœur même de l'Incarnation.[39]

---

[37] Ibid., p. 615.
[38] Ibid.
[39] *Œuvre poétique,* "Notes," pp. 1521-1522.

Thus, by the mediation of the present Péguy arrives at the central mystery of Christianity. As Paul Cimon observes in *Péguy et le Temps présent*: "La conception péguyiste du présent se situe, en effet, au cœur même de l'Incarnation, c'est-à-dire, au cœur même de cette insertion toujours vivante 'du spirituel dans le charnel' et de 'l'éternel dans le temporel.' " [40]

In the "Argument" of *L'Esprit et l'Eau,* Claudel spoke of his vision of Eternity in transitory creation. The poet suddenly becomes aware that the two aspects of reality are inseparable. God is in and of the world.

> Vous êtes ici.
> Vous êtes ici et je ne puis pas être autre part qu'avec vous.
> Que m'arrive-t-il? car c'est comme si ce vieux monde était maintenant fermé.
> Comme jadis lorsqu'apportée du ciel la tête au-dessus du temple
> La clé de voûte vint capter la forêt païenne
> O mon Dieu, je la vois, la clef maintenant qui délivre
> Ce n'est point celle qui ouvre, mais celle-là qui ferme! [41]

Péguy uses this same sort of "closed temple" metaphor in *Le Mystère des Saints innocents.* The arch which ascends to the vaulted summit of creation is the Old Testament. Carnal and temporal, it originates on earth and ascends. The arch which meets it is the New Testament, beginning in eternity, descending to earth, spiritual and eternal. At the apex and joining the two, is Jesus incarnate:

> Et la clef de cette mystique voûte.
> La clef elle-même
> Charnelle, spirituelle,
> Temporelle, éternelle,
> C'est Jésus,
> Homme
> Dieu. [42]

In this mystic union, hope at last becomes possible.

---

[40] Paul Cimon, *Péguy et le Temps présent* (Montréal: Fides, 1964), p. 13.
[41] *L'Esprit et l'Eau,* p. 240.
[42] *Le Mystère des Saints innocents,* p. 784.

Louis Gillet wrote of *Le Porche de la Deuxième Vertu*:

> Tout le poème n'est qu'une cantate et un hymne à la joie. Le poète y va de tout son cœur et de toutes ses ressources, il nage dans une félicité sans bornes, dans une sorte d'océan de lyrisme sans plages. Quel contraste avec la contrainte, la tonalité sourde, l'atmosphère accablée du *Mystère de la Charité*.[43]

How far Péguy had come in his long pilgrimage from the man who, in "Encore de la Grippe" had told his doctor: "Et quand on se fonde sur l'immensité de l'espérance éternelle pour me consoler de la prochaine épouvante, je refuse. Non pas que l'inquiétude et l'angoisse ne me soit douloureuse, mais mieux vaut encore une inquiétude ou même une épouvante sincère qu'une espérance religieuse."[44]

No one knows for sure exactly when Péguy found his faith. The Tharaud brothers affectionately observe that no man could have chosen the battlegrounds Péguy chose, or have defended Dreyfus in the way in which he did, without making himself very pleasing to the Almighty. One thing is certain, it was a very long journey, and one cannot speak of any particular moment of "conversion," as in the case of Claudel. The latter had hesitated a year before confiding his change of heart to his family. Péguy kept his secret even longer, fearful of offending the determined atheism of Madame Baudoin as well as startling, even alienating his subscribers. Besides, in his way of thinking, his return to the Church was tantamount to a break of faith with his wife, to whom he was united by civil ceremony only.

In 1908 he confided to Lotte that he had become a Catholic, but the journey had surely begun earlier and was by no means completed. Three years later, in "Un Nouveau Théologien: M. Laudet," Péguy would describe the change in himself as a very gradual process, achieved by going forward, never back. His son, Marcel, confirms this: "Mon père n'est pas revenu au catholicisme vers 1908, mais il est venu... en partant de la philosophie grecque."[45] He attributes his father's conversion to two factors: his association,

---

[43] Gillet, p. 184.
[44] "Encore de la Grippe," II, pp. 156-157.
[45] *Lettres et Entretiens*, p. 46.

through writing, with his beloved saints, Jeanne, saint Louis, ... with Polyeucte, and his personal experience with God.

From the beginning Péguy had been sorely troubled by the idea of damnation which was probably the underlying cause for his rejection of Christian doctrine. Jeanne is preoccupied with damnation throughout the 1897 work. *Le Mystère de la Charité* postdates his confession to Lotte, but still we find this revolt against the idea of Hell. One can feel Péguy's antipathy toward Madame Gervaise — does she here represent established religion? — whom he casts in a thankless role. To Jeannette's anguished "Alors, madame Gervaise, quand vous voyez qu'une âme se damne..." she can only respond with the inadequate palliative, "Les voies de Dieu sont insondables." [46] Jeannette bids her a brusque "Adieu," and Madame Gervaise leaves. But Péguy added by hand on the proofs, "Madame Gervaisse était sortie. Mais elle rentre avant que l'on ait eu le temps de baisser le rideau." [47] The discussion, then, was not closed.

In *Le Porche,* in those passages already cited, Péguy finally understood that it was man, not God, who might fail both himself and his Creator. However the operation was accomplished in his mind, it was accomplished once and for all. And important turning point in his inner life had been reached:

> ... Sa vie se retrouva, arrachée aux flots du temps, fondée en l'éternité du présent (oui, c'était bien toujours ce gouffre de "l'immédiat," selon Bergson; — mais le gouffre s'était rempli de lumière, et c'était Dieu qui était "présent.") [48]

wrote Romain Rolland of this point. The man who told Clio, "Il sait que *l'on* n'est pas heureux," could add, in the same paragraph:

> Or, voyez l'inconséquence. Le même homme. Cet homme a naturellement un fils de quatorze ans. Il n'a qu'une pensée. C'est que son fils soit heureux ... C'est une pensée de bête. [49]

But the muse of history answers him:

---

[46] *Le Mystère de la Charité,* p. 525.
[47] Ibid.
[48] Rolland, II, p. 207.
[49] "Clio." II, p. 229.

> Or je dis que rien n'est aussi touchant que cette perpétuelle, que cette éternelle, que cette éternelle renaissante inconséquence; et que rien n'est aussi beau; et que rien n'est aussi désarmant devant Dieu; et c'est ici la commune merveille de votre jeune Espérance.[50]

In the figure of the Virgin, too, Péguy could now find great comfort — "Car le fils a pris tous les péchés. Mais la Mère a pris toutes les douleurs."[51] In *Le Porche* he writes of a peasant father whose children become sick. Terror-struck and unable to bear the anxiety, he decides upon an audacious move. He confides his sick children, through prayer, to the Virgin, not asking but demanding her help: "Prenez-les. Je vous les donne. Faites-en ce que vous voudrez. / J'en ai assez."[52] And of course, the children get well.

In 1912 what had been written as poetry became fact. His son, Pierre, contracted typhoid and was close to death. Péguy, like the peasant, gave his child to the Virgin, vowing to make a pilgrimage on foot to Chartres should the child recover. * And, as in the poem, his son passed safely through the crisis. Significantly, the "interior act" of the poem preceded the act in real life. In 1913 Péguy wrote to Lotte:

> Notre Dame m'a sauvé du désespoir. C'était le plus grand danger. Des gens comme nous ont toujours autant de foi et autant de charité qu'il faut. Mais c'est l'espoir qui peut manquer. J'en suis sorti en écrivant mon Porche.[53]

With the *Porche* Péguy was at last able to emerge from the shadows of despair into the sunlight of hope. He had found it in the very present Incarnation of Christ, in the gentle image of the Virgin. And hope indeed transfigures his last poetic writings, unifying them and giving them a sort of luminosity his earlier work had

---

[50] Ibid.
[51] *Le Porche*, p. 558.
[52] Ibid.
* Péguy did indeed make two pilgrimages to Chartres, which have since been duplicated by thousands of people annually, on June 14, 1912, and on July 25, 1913 (v. Feuillets de l'Amitié Charles Péguy, no. 5, juillet 1949, pp. 4-13).
[53] *Lettres et Entretiens*, p. 171.

lacked. It would be for him the fragile bud on the giant oak of faith, or the little girl who says her prayers and sleeps well. Hope meant renewal. And it was by renewal, by a return to the source that Péguy would try to rescue the poor, tired, modern world from stultification.

Chapter IV

THE ONCE AND FUTURE WORLD

> Il n'y a rien pour quoi l'homme soit moins fait
> que le bonheur et dont il se lasse aussi vite.
> *Le Soulier de Satin*

While both Claudel and Péguy were drawn to the Middle Ages, neither was making a spiritual retreat; both were instead seeking some kind of prescription for the contemporary world. In a poem dedicated to Saint Francis Claudel writes: "Ce n'est pas François tellement par lui-même qui m'intéresse, et laissons là si vous voulez bien le XIII° siècle et Assise et Bernadone,"[1] and goes on to say that what exists for all time is Saint Francis, witness in the presence of God, or, in other words, the *essence* of the saint. He spells this out even more clearly in a lecture he gave concerning his long "Sainte Geneviève."

> La Geneviève que je voulais décrire, ce n'est pas seulement celle qui a arrêté Attila, c'est celle qui a barré la route sur la Marne aux Huns de 1914. Il fallait donc mettre la sainte tout près de nous, montrer que pour en retrouver les traits nous n'avons qu'à regarder les visages chéris de ces femmes, de ces mères et de ces sœurs qui nous entourent.[2]

In a second lecture, and referring to the same poem, he said:

> On pourrait appeler *Sainte Geneviève* la mobilisation sous le feu de l'ennemi d'une imagination française. Tous les

---

[1] "Saint François," p. 912.
[2] *Œuvre poétique*, "Notes," p. 1138.

souvenirs de l'enfance et du pays natal, en arrière tous les évènements de l'histoire nationale étroitement réunis par le retour d'un même danger, ce vaste mouvement d'une nation qui se désagrège et se regroupe autour de ses forces essentielles et vitales, tout cela en moi se levait et se mettait en marche à la fois . . .[3]

A good part of Claudel's poetic and theatrical production directly concerns persons, real or fictional, who lived during the Middle Ages; *L'Announce faite à Marie, Le Soulier de Satin,* the *Corona Benignitatis Anni Dei, Feuilles de Saints* (containing the important "Ode Jubilaire" dedicated to Dante), *Visages radieux* (which treats many of Péguy's favorite saints), *Poèmes et Paroles durant la Guerre de Trente Ans,* and the beautiful *Jeanne d'Arc au Bucher,* to mention only the more important works. Yet, just as Claudel shows little interest in the St. Francis of the thirteenth century, so his concern is not an historical period generally (and loosely) known as the Middle Ages, but certain attitudes which, taken together, seem to him at least to form the *essence* of medieval life, temporal and spiritual.

It is one thing to point out what in this period appealed to Claudel, quite another to determine why. As we've seen Claudel owes much to St. Thomas Aquinas, whose metaphysics are at the bases of *Art poétique,* and by extension, of his entire thought structure. But a writer is not influenced by chance. He rejects and he chooses. He even preempts ideas, values, systems to which he, by his own temperament and life experience, is attuned. If Claudel writes of medieval saints and heroes, or if he places his own imaginative creations within the Middle Ages, it is because there is a profound coincidence between the individual and collective values of those people and times and Claudel's own.

There were, in short, certain spiritual, social and intellectual attitudes associated with the Middle Ages which Claudel admired, or with which he felt a deep empathy. Sometimes this admiration was rather superficial — a sort of emotional nostalgia that did not really have anything to do with more profound aspects of the poet's nature. For example, he admired the supposed "simplicity" of the Middle Ages, and in some of his own poems sought to emulate it.

---

[3] Ibid., p. 1141.

Such attempts ran counter to both his talent and temperament. On the other hand he was genuinely fascinated by medieval ceremony, in the sense of both pageantry and rite. It was love of ceremony, after all, that brought a dilettante to Notre Dame de Paris that Christmas of 1886. His poetic purpose would be to reproduce the divine ceremony in his work as it had been reproduced in life, and in life's counterpart, art, throughout the Middle Ages.

The other-world orientation of the medieval period struck a responsive note in Claudel, who would make of his own life a continual contemplation and reiteration of the Eternal. But this orientation also fostered the belief, illumined through Christ's example and the legends of the martyrs, of the efficacy of suffering. Claudel's life experience tended to validate such an attitude, which pervades his theater and his poetry. The theme of suffering, moreover, is intimately bound to the figure and role of woman, which, in turn, is linked to his concept of love and marriage.

Woman plays a paramount if ambiguous role in Claudel's work. She is, as he states, "la Vierge, la Sagesse, l'Eglise, l'Ame," but she is also — as he does *not* state — the temptress, Eve ... Isolde. The same poet who created Violaine, the Princess, Prouhèze, also gave us Mara, Lûmir, Sichel. At first glance it might seem as though Claudel were merely repeating, after his own fashion, the Augustinian observation that a woman sent man to his destruction and a woman opened the way to his salvation. Certainly the medieval church at once raised woman to her highest pinnacle, in the cult of the Virgin, and at the same time shared the apostle Paul's distrust of her. Claudel, like Dante, appears to be most interested in woman as an agent of salvation, and Dante's influence, though expressly denied by the former, is most apparent in Violaine and Prouhèze. But how does one explain Ysé (*Le Partage*) or Lala (*La Ville*)? Both are unfaithful to their marriage vows, both desert husband and child, yet each seems to hold out a promise — ambiguous as it is — of some kind of redemption. Here, I think, we encounter another medieval tradition, separate though not entirely divorced from the religious: the concept of courtly love, as it was refined through the poetry of the *troubadours* and *trouvères*. An idealized form of *l'amour courtois* raised love, generally outside of marriage, to an absolute value, and put woman on a pseudo-religious pedestal, beautiful, exigeant, often unattainable.

All of these attitudes form a cluster within the closed world of the Middle Ages. We have seen how Claudel, after his four year long battle with the angel, capitulated, and set about building a new edifice which could hold the faith that had been almost thrust upon him. The symbols for this house or closure are several, the most perfect being the circle. An important medieval symbol, the circle was to Claudel the form of forms. As there is a coincidence between certain medieval attitudes and Claudel's, so too there is between the content and form of his work and the God whom philosophers of the Middle Ages defined as a sphere, the center of which is everywhere, the circumference, nowhere.

That Claudel was moved by the naivete and apparent simplicity of medieval life and art is evinced in his appreciation of Gothic architecture, or his evocation of the simple life of Villeneuve. Just as Péguy felt that a child raised in Orléans had literally touched *ancienne France,* Claudel believed that the course of life in the little village had changed hardly at all over the centuries. As he wrote to Gide, he longed to breathe the "bienheureuse ignorance" of an earlier time. Yet this longing for simplicity does not seem to correspond to his deeper psychological and religious needs. When Claudel tries to be simple, either in content or form, one gets the impression of a genie squeezed into a bottle, and most impatient to be loosed. Compare, for example, the short poems in *Visages radieux* with the much longer ones in *Feuilles de Saints,* both of which works deal with many of the same figures. In *Visages radieux* we find a very short (eleven line) poem describing Saint Martin. It might well have been inspired by one of the statues decorating a Gothic facade, which portray a particular saint in an attitude associated with his legend. Claudel relates the incident, recounted in *Lives of the Saints,* in which Saint Martin, the only one in a crowd to take pity on a freezing beggar, cuts his cloak in two and shares it with him. The poem ends with a little moral, rather in the style of a fable. By contrast, the "Saint Martin" of *Feuilles de Saints* is a complex, amply developed poem, in which Claudel deals not with the legend but the "essence" of the saint — the Christian soldier whose spirit inspires the French army to repulse and ultimately to defeat the Germans. Unlike the short poem, this one contains many of Claudel's favorite themes. There is the striving to grasp the Eternal, even if momentarily, already found in the *Odes*: "Cela vaut la peine d'être éternel, ne serait-ce qu'une minute!" [4] and the indissoluble union of the spiritual and corporal: "C'est heureux pour ces pauvres gens," dit St. Martin, "Que je ne sois tout de même un pur esprit." [5] The house image reappears, this time as the castle of the soul: "Malgré la guerre et l'orage, on m'a dit que ce grand château de l'âme avec Dieu aujourd'hui même est possible." [6] The error — or sin — of the Germans is that of Tête d'Or — "Peuple mal baptisé, en as-tu assez maintenant de ce grossier désir d'être Dieu?" [7] And again like Tête d'Or, their energies, spurred by despair, are directed toward self-annihilation: "C'est l'enthousiasme de la mort qui t'a pris, comme d'autres l'espérance!"

The "little poem" of *Visages radieux* simply is not suited to Claudel's talents. There is a love of pageantry, ceremony, a need for expansion in him that refuses to be restricted either vertically — in stanza length — or horizontally — by verse line. In an interesting lecture which he gave on *Feuilles de Saints* he takes issue with proponents of the short poem, exquisite as some such poems may be:

> ...Au plus beau des poèmes courts, il manquera toujours ce qui est le domaine le plus élevé de l'art, la composition, la proportion à un vaste ensemble qui relève infiniment chaque détail et lui donne toute sa valeur... à mon avis, le but de l'art est la recherche des ensembles, des grandes masses régies par une puissante composition dont tel saillant plus heureux n'est que l'un des effets particuliers. [8]

Only in a work of the ample scope of *Feuilles de Saints* can Claudel fulfill his self-imposed task, set out in *Art poétique*:

> L'acte par lequel l'homme atteste la permanence des choses, par lequel, *en dehors du temps,* en dehors des circonstances et causes secondes, *il formule l'ensemble des conditions permanentes dont la réunion donne à chaque chose son droit de devenir présente à l'esprit,* par lequel il la conçoit dans

---

[4] *Feuilles de Saints*, p. 668.
[5] Ibid., p. 669.
[6] Ibid.
[7] Ibid., p. 671.
[8] *Œuvre poétique*, "Notes," p. 1129.

> son cœur et répète l'ordre qui l'a créée, s'appelle la parole.[9]
> [italics added]

Put another way, Claudel repeats or re-creates the saints, making them present to the contemporary world. Thus, November 11, which marked the signing of the armistice, was also a triumph for Saint Martin, whose feast day is the same date. For Saint Martin *is,* and his essential self continues to exist.

The *Corona Benignitatis Anni Dei* is another example of such a re-creation. In fact, Claudel had originally planned to divide his work following the divisions of the missal. In a letter to Gide he described the collection of poems "... qui sera non point une imitation du bréviare, mais un cycle de chants naissant sous les pas des heures sacrées,"[10] and in a lecture given on the work, explained, "Jai voulu montrer au-dessus de l'année terrestre et marchant du même pas, une autre année, celle du Ciel, celle du Calendrier dont l'étincelante couronne et la guirlande toujours recommençant sur l'immutable itinéraire dont le Christ fixé les étapes, nous introduisent à l'éternel office."[11] Here the inspiration was directly medieval, for he wished to compose a series of liturgical hymns in the tradition of the sequences of Notker, Adam de Saint-Victor and Prudentius.

Ceremony, then, appealed to Claudel on both an emotional and intellectual level. It allowed scope and amplitude for his own peculiar talents, which were far less effective in restricted and restrictive forms. Symbolically, through re-creation and repetition of the Eternal, his work prefigured his role in Paradise, the accomplishment of his own part in the eternal celebration of the Office.

It was in part at least the other-world orientation of the Middle Ages which led to the emphasis on the value of suffering and renunciation, two aspects of a single theme that appears constantly in Claudel's work. In *The Age of Faith* Will Durant examines the reasons for this orientation:

> To understand the Middle Ages we must forget our modern rationalism, our proud confidence in reason and science, our restless search after wealth and power and an earthly par-

---

[9] *Art poétique,* p. 194.
[10] *Correspondance,* Claudel, Gide, p. 89.
[11] *Œuvre poétique,* "Notes," p. 1092.

adise; we must enter sympathetically into the mood of men disillusioned of these pursuits, standing at the end of a thousand years of rationalism, finding all dreams of utopia shattered by war and proverty and barbarism, seeking consolation in the hope of happiness beyond the grave, inspired and comforted by the story and figure of Christ . . . [12]

Such an attitude permitted men, not merely to rationalize earthly suffering, but to exalt it as a positive value. Suffering became a means of purification and ultimate redemption. Humiliation of the body and bodily desires freed the soul for closer communication with the spiritual, for, as Mara (*L'Annonce*) observes, "Il est facile d'être une sainte quand la lèpre nous sert d'appoint." [13]

Claudel had little faith in rationalism or so-called scientific progress. Events in his own life tended to orient him toward another, better world. God's rejection of him as a monk, for example, painful as it may have been at the time, had opened his eyes to his true role as poet-priest. Certainly the violent love he had conceived for "Rose" on the *Ernest-Simons* strengthened this attitude. That a love so profound should be beyond the law — his own chosen law — was terribly hard to accept, yet he would come to feel that the wound had been a necessary one, opening him to the full meaning of spiritual love. *

Moreover, even apart from these experiences, Claudel seems to have been temperamentally predisposed toward such an attitude. There is evidence in his early works of an ascetic — to use the religious term — or masochistic — if one prefers the psychological — element in the poet's nature which later events in his life only tended to confirm. In the first (1892) version of *La Jeune Fille Violaine*, Violaine, for no apparent reason, voluntarily gives up Baube (Jacques) to Bibiane (Mara). Paul-André Lesort, in *Claudel par lui-même*, recognized the subtle danger in the early play. Referring to this particular point, he wrote: "L'œuvre évoque une menace autant qu'un appel." [14] Violaine has no love for her sister, nor

---

[12] Will Durant, *The Age of Faith* (N.Y.: Simon and Schuster, 1950), p. 74.
[13] *L'Annonce*, II, p. 72.
* For evidence of the evolution of Claudel's thinking in this regard, see the discussion later in this chapter regarding the revised version of *Partage de Midi*, particularly as regards the "Cantique de Mésa."
[14] Paul-André Lesort, *Claudel par lui-même* (Paris: Ed. du Seuil, 1965), p. 36.

does she feel the spiritual thirst of the later Violaine. Her attitude is really that of the ascetic who rejoices in sacrifice for the sake of sacrifice. In the second version there is still some of this spiritual self-flagellation: "... ce sacrifice m'a paru si cruel, si aimable, que je n'ai su me garder de le faire." [15] Even in *L'Annonce,* the longing for martyrdom is only thinly veiled in Violaine's words to Mara: "Le mâle est prêtre, mais il n'est pas défendu à la femme d'être victime." [16]

If the longing to make a sacrifice of oneself is better disguised in later versions, it is probable that the Catholic intellectual became aware of dangers of which the poet had been unconscious. Violaine, Prouhèze, *et al* were made to fit into a certain scheme, and their sacrifice, if voluntarily embraced, would have a firmer theological basis. Still, in the following discussion it is helpful to remember that we are dealing with a man who, in 1908, wrote: "Toute rose pour moi est peu au prix de son épine! / Peu de chose pour moi l'amour où manque la souffrance divine!" [17]

And suffering is, in fact, a constant in Claudel's theater. Sometimes it takes a physical form — the crucifixion of the Princess or of Rodrigue's brother, the Jesuit priest, Tête d'Or's mutilation, Violaine's leprosy. More often, however, it is a spiritual thing, and involves the sacrifice or renunciation of the character's deepest desires. Renunciation is, in fact, intimately linked to Claudel's concept of the role of woman.

It may be helpful to digress a moment to examine briefly Claudel's concept of evil, for suffering is surely an apparent evil. As noted, Claudel had begun in 1900 to study St. Thomas Aquinas intensively. Now, for St. Thomas, evil is not a quality as such, but merely the absence of good, as cold is the absence of heat. In God's unknowable plan, it may be the means to the accomplishment of some greater good. This belief on Claudel's part accounts for what I would term the "rehabilitation of Mara," who in the earliest play is Evil incarnate. Later, however, she becomes the unwitting instrument of Violaine's "beatification." As Violaine herself tells her, "Mara, tu as coupé le lien qui me tenait, et je ne repose plus que

---

[15] *La Jeune Fille Violaine,* I, p. 630.
[16] *L'Annonce,* II, p. 74.
[17] "Hymne du Sacré Cœur," p. 407.

dans la main de Dieu même." [18] When Jacques, referring to Mara, tells Violaine, "Il faut bien qu'elle vous ait haïe!" [19] Violaine corrects him impatiently, "Homme égoïste et méchant! mais 'il faut qu'elle m'ait bien aimée.'" [20] That is why she can bless the hand which guided her to the sand pit and death. Even more explicitly, she credits Mara with having a part in the miracle of Aubaine's rebirth. When Jacques asks, "Qui donc lui a rendu la vie?" Violaine replies, "Dieu seul, et avec Dieu / La foi et le désespoir de sa mère." [21] After her sister's death Mara explains in a most curious way her value to Jacques. Only she can cause him hurt and sorrow, she says, and then adds, "Et je suis la sœur de Violaine." [22] The emphasis on their kinship — their complementary roles — is made clear by the coordinating conjunction, *et*.

That this problem of evil was a concern to Claudel is evident from a remark he once made concerning Gide (in reference to *Les Caves du Vatican*) which mystified the latter: *Le mal ne compose pas*. Dominique Arban during an interview asked what was meant by this expression. Claudel's reply is illuminating and unequivocal:

> Mais, d'après la théologie, le mal n'existe pas. C'est un élément destructif qui n'est que négation. Le mal n'est intéressant que parce qu'il s'accompagne de souffrance. A ce point là, c'est un élément créateur incontestable. [23]

Such an attitude explains an apparent paradox in *Le Repos du septième Jour*. The emperor observes that "Le Mal est ce qui n'est pas," [24] but then he continues: "Mais du moins il est un mal que tout homme vivant redoute: la souffrance. / Il lui a été donné de souffrir, et cette indication n'est pas vaine: / Par là il est capable d'apprendre et de se corriger." [25] Thus suffering, while an apparent evil, is a blessing in disguise, since it is a means of purification and ultimate redemption, both individual and collective. Just as Violaine

---

[18] *Violaine*, I, p. 618.
[19] Ibid., p. 632.
[20] Ibid.
[21] *L'Annonce*, II, p. 92.
[22] Ibid., p. 102.
[23] *Correspondance*, Claudel, Gide, p. 249.
[24] *Le Repos du Septième Jour*, II, p. 824.
[25] Ibid., p. 825.

had urged Pierre to be worthy of the flame which was consuming him, so she afterwards dedicates herself to the same fate, explaining her role to Mara: "Le bois où l'on a mis le feu ne donne pas de la cendre seulement mais une flamme aussi," [26] and then, elaborating the flame metaphor:

> Dieu est avare et ne permet qu'aucune créature soit allumée,
> Sans qu'un peu d'impureté s'y consume,
> La sienne ou celle qui l'entoure, comme la braise de l'encensoir qu'on attise!
> Et certes le malheur de ce temps est grand.
> Ils n'ont point de père. Ils regardent et ne savent plus
>   où est le Roi et le Pape.
> C'est pourquoi, voici mon corps en travail à la place de
>   la chrétienté qui se dissout.
> Puissante est la souffrance quand elle est aussi volontaire
>   que le péché. [27]

Also, when suffering is voluntarily accepted, it is inextricably linked with joy. When, in *L'Otage*, Sygne at last capitulates before Monsieur Badilon and accepts her immolation, he rejoices with her: "Voici la creature avec son Createur *dans l'Eden de la croix!*" [28] *

---

[26] *L'Annonce*, II, p. 74.
[27] Ibid., p. 75.
[28] *L'Otage*, II, p. 272.

* This play, incidentally, illustrates an aspect of Claudel's attraction for the Middle Ages which will be examined more fully, and in a slightly different context, in the conclusion of this chapter — i.e., his longing for some higher authority which could provide a code of behavior within a closed system. Always a monarchist at heart, he regretted the attrition and final dissolution of royal authority, as well as that of feudalism which had helped support this authority. (Notice, in this connection, Anne's reference to the King and the Pontiff.) The victory of Turelure in *L'Otage* marked the end of the rule of the landed aristocracy and signified the triumph of bourgeois mediocrity. As Georges de Coufontaine observes, "Les temps de la foi sont finis, maintenant recommence la servitude de l'homme a l'homme..." Notice with what nostalgia Claudel recalls these earlier days. Georges pledges his troth to Sygne after the fashion of a medieval knight, by giving her his gauntlet. Sygne, for her part, is almost as concerned about her name and honor as Roland; in fact, when she dies she tries, like Roland, to hold out her glove to Saint Michel. When Badilon urges her sacrifice, she replies in terms which recall the ancient feudal contract, "Que Dieu fasse son devoir de son côté, comme je fais le mien." (p. 265). It is significant that the name of Coufontaine will be debased, though not destroyed, as it passes not to Georges' offspring, but to Turelure and his son.

[italics added]. Or when, in *Le Père Humilié*, Pensée protests to Orian, "Nous ne voulons pas de la souffrance," [29] the latter counters with "Vous ne voulez donc de la joie." [30] Probably nowhere are both the redemptive value of suffering and the accompanying joy more clearly stated than in the last version of *L'Announce*, by Anne:

> Elle est morte. Ma femme aussi
> Est morte, la sainte Pucelle
> A été brulée et jetée au vent, pas un de ses os ne reste
>   à la terre.
> Mais le Roi et le Pontife de nouveau sont rendus à la France
>   et à l'univers.
> . . .
> Est-ce que le but de la vie est de vivre? est-ce que les
>   pieds des enfants de Dieu seront attachés à cette terre
>   miserable?
> Il n'est pas de vivre, mais de mourir, et non point charpenter
>   la croix mais d'y monter, et de donner ce que nous avons en
>   riant!
> Là est la joie, là est la liberté, là la grâce, là la jeunesse
>   éternelle! [31]

Let us examine now in more detail that special expression of suffering — renunciation — in its relation to the function of woman in Claudel's theater, for, as I have pointed out, the two themes are closely linked. True, the act of renunciation may occasionally be initiated by the man, or it may be mutual, but far more frequently it is the woman's decision, or she, at least, is the more conscious of the necessity of the sacrifice. There is, I think, a fundamental contradiction here — between what Claudel wants to believe and what he feels — which affects the role of woman in his plays; a contradiction he tries, in a very interesting way, to solve. Nevertheless the conflict seems to remain, and can perhaps help explain some of the paradoxes and difficulties of his theater.

Claudel appears to have been predisposed toward the ascetic. Violaine, describing her sacrifice as at once *cruel* and *aimable* — a striking alliance of unlike terms — reveals a certain fascination for

---

[29] *Le Père humilié*, II, p. 508.
[30] Ibid.
[31] *L'Annonce*, II, p. 105.

self-immolation. Claudel's detailed critique of Gide's *La Porte étroite* is illuminating in this respect. The book, dealing as it does with the deliberate renunciation of love and happiness, appealed strongly to Claudel, and when he deals with it as a work of art, his praise is unqualified:

> Comme œuvre d'art, il n'y a rien à dire, tout est logique d'un bout à l'autre. La grossière littérature du siècle dernier donne le change sur l'étude des sentiments les plus profonds. *Non, la satisfaction sexuelle n'est pas celle de la passion et d'amour, elle en est un rétrécissement parfois caricatural, une déformation le plus souvent et toujours une transformation.* Il ne s'agit pas la de finesse platonicienne. *Le sentiment de "refus" est profondément caché au cœur de la femme,* on le retrouve même dans les espèces animales! Il n'y a pas sujet de drame plus riche et plus complexe, il n'y en a qui soit plus pathétique pour une âme masculine, de là l'interêt pour nous de tous ces livres où nous assistons à la lutte de la passion contre le devoir... La force de votre livre, c'est qu'il n'y a pas de devoir extérieur, mais seulement une voix intime.[32]

But when Claudel criticizes Gide's work from a theological point of view he finds it wanting (and contradicts himself!). Precisely the aspect which fascinates the artist — that Alissa has no exterior duty — troubles the Catholic. He finds in *La Porte étroite* "une douceur dantesque, mais avec, au-dessous, quelque chose de terriblement amer, je n'ose dire de désespéré," [33] and he reproaches Gide of quietism.

For Claudel, the Catholic, the sacrifice, because it is so painful, must also be justifiable: *It must be shown to be both necessary and useful*. To examine several instances:

Anne without warning decides to leave his home and family, to set off on a pilgrimage to the Holy Land. "Je suis las d'être heureux," he exclaims, and then continues:

Tout périt et je suis épargné
En sorte que je paraîtrai devant Lui vide et sans titre,
   entre ceux qui ont reçu leur récompense.

---

[32] *Correspondance*, Claudel, Gide, p. 101.
[33] Ibid.

...
Lequel reçoit davantage, le vase plein, ou vide?
Et laquelle a besoin de plus d'eau, la citerne ou la source? [34]

He renounces his happiness because his very plenitude will operate against him in the final Judgment: his "wholeness" leaves no room for God, and without the thirst (*le vase vide*) he would not search out the spiritual source.

The idea of the danger of happiness is exemplified, in a more complex fashion, in the case of Orian in *Le Père humilié*. Both Orian and Orso, his younger brother, love the blind Pensée, who loves Orian. Since neither brother wishes to deprive the other of his happiness they seek the Pope's counsel. Orso admits to the Pope that Pensée does not love him: still, he sees this as no real objection, for he is confident that he can win her affection through patience and kindness. At the same time he assures the Pope that, should he lose Pensée, he would hardly die of grief: "Je ne mourrai que si on me casse la tête et il y faudra un bon coup! / Ce n'est pas une petite fille qui privera d'un officier les armées de la Sainte Eglise." [35] This measured response is in direct contrast to Orian's profound, impassioned adoration, and for that very reason the Pope decides for Orso! "Pauvre petit," he tells Orian, "tu l'aimes trop." When Orso protests that this seems a strange reason for depriving Orian of Pensée, the Pope apparently contradicts himself: "Ce n'est pas parce qu'il l'aime trop, mais parce qu'il ne l'aime pas assez. / ...Ce n'est pas aimer quelqu'un que de ne pas lui donner ce qu'on a en soi de meilleur." [36] Orso is mystified, but Orian understands:

> Orso, si je l'épousais, il n'y a point de mesure possible
>   entre nous;
> Ce qu'elle demande, je ne peux le lui donner.
> C'est mon âme qu'elle demande, et je ne peux absolument
>   pas la lui donner,
> Moi-même ne la possédant pas. [37]

In a long farewell scene Orian and Pensée probe the depths and nature of their love. Pensée feels that she was quite literally

---

[34] *L'Annonce*, II, p. 31.
[35] *Le Père humilié*, II, p. 525.
[36] Ibid.
[37] Ibid., p. 526.

made *for* and *of* Orian: "Quand on vous préparait, Orian, je pense qu'il restait un peu de substances qui avait été disposée en vous, et c'est de cela que vous manquez et que je fus faite." [38] It is because Orian knows this to be true that he renounces Pensée's love, for some other fate, of which he is yet only dimly aware, is prepared for him:

> Il est nécessaire que je ne sois pas un heureux! Il est nécessaire que je ne sois pas un satisfait!
> Il est nécessaire que l'on ne me bouche pas la bouche et les yeux avec cette espèce de bonheur qui nous ôte le désir
>
> ...Pensée, vous êtes le danger pour moi.
> La grande aventure vers la lumière, le diamant quelque part, il est nécessaire que j'en sois seul. [39]

There are two separate and distinct reasons why Orian must renounce Pensée. First, the sort of love he demands transcends any earthly — and sexual — union ("C'est toujours le même calembour banal, la même coupe tout de site vidée," [40] he says of this kind of love) and he explains to her, "Ce que je te demandais, ce que je voulais te donner, cela n'est pas compatible avec le temps, mais avec l'éternité." [41] Second, and even more importantly, if their love could be consummated they would form, as it were, a *whole*. This, of course, is what Pensée sensed when she said she was made of the part left out of Orian, and is exactly the same idea that Anne had expressed through the metaphor of the empty cup. Satisfied by Pensée, Orian would have no need to look further for "le diamant quelque part."

It is a significant insofar as woman's role is concerned that although Orian initiated the sacrifice, Pensée does not merely acquiesce. It is she who makes the definitive decision. Orian weakens and says he will stay at a word from her, but she replies, "Adieu donc" and when he reiterates, "Pensée, ah, je resterai avec toi si tu veux," she reproaches him: "Ne dis pas des choses indignes." [42]

---

[38] Ibid., p. 537.
[39] Ibid., p. 534.
[40] Ibid., p. 537.
[41] Ibid., p. 542.
[42] Ibid., p. 543.

Their love can only be perfected in absence, and finally, in death. As Orian says, "Quand je vous ai quittée, Pensée, c'est alors que vous vous êtes emparée de moi," [43] and "Si je meurs, Pensée, c'est que sans doute il n'y avait aucun autre moyen pour moi de pénétrer jusqu'à vous! " [44]

Jacques Duron in his article, "Le Mythe de Tristan," has accurately described such love:

> ... Ce désir irrésistible qui fait qu'un homme et une femme sont mus l'un vers l'autre comme vers leur béatitude, c'est ce même désir qui les attire de ce qu'ils sont l'un pour l'autre, donc au plus haut d'eux-mêmes, et qui dès lors noue entre eux une relation telle qu'elle ne pourra se parfaire en deça de leur propre perfection. D'où l'idée du sacrifice, inséparable de l'exigence d'un amour total. [45]

The renunciation of love results in what is variously described as a "thirst," a "wound," an "emptiness" left in the sufferer. The sense of emptiness is essential, in Claudel's view, to man's highest accomplishment: "Le vide est une condition essentielle du mouvement et de la vie." [46]

This is what Pierre means when he quotes the Beatitude, "Blessed are they which do hunger and thirst," to Violaine. Wounded, thirsting through her agency — "O image de la Beauté éternelle, tu n'es pas à moi" [47] — he will seek relief in God's service. Moreover, he realizes that like himself, Violaine can only be "completed" by divine love: "Qui êtes-vous, jeune fille, et quelle est donc cette part que Dieu en vous s'est réservée . . . ?" [48] Violaine recognizes this herself when she pleads with Jacques to take her entirely, but Jacques does not understand her meaning until after her death, when he can at last see, "Dieu ne me l'aurait pas prise, si elle avait été remplie de moi tout entière, ne laissant aucune place vide / 'La part de Dieu' comme l'appellent les bonnes femmes." [49]

---

[43] Ibid., p. 536.
[44] Ibid., p. 539.
[45] Jacques Duron, "Le Mythe de Tristan," *Hommage à Paul Claudel*, NRF, Ed. spéciale (Paris: Gallimard, 1955), p. 549.
[46] Œuvres complètes, XXIV, *L'Evangile d'Isaïe*, p. 13.
[47] *L'Annonce*, II, p. 13.
[48] Ibid., II, p. 13.
[49] Ibid., p. 91.

In each case, the renunciation of love in life results in salvation after death. Nowhere is this more plainly enunciated then in *Le Soulier de Satin*. The guardian angel of Prouhèze explains to the letter that she is "bait" to catch Rodrigue for God: "Cet orgueilleux, il n'y avait pas d'autre moyen de lui faire comprendre le prochain, de le lui entrer dans la chair; / Il n'y avait pas d'autre moyen de lui faire comprendre la dépendance, la nécessité et le besoin..."[50] And the angel comforts Prouhèze, telling her that though she must remain separated in life from Rodrigue, she is the instrument of his redemption. Moreover, after death they will be eternally united. Only then, Prouhèze will have been transformed:

> Non point cette vilaine et disgracieuse création au bout
>   de ma ligne, non point ce triste poisson.
> ...
> Prouhèze, ma sœur, cette enfant de Dieu dans la lumière
>   que je salue.
> Cette Prouhèze que voient les Anges, c'est celle-là sans
>   le savoir qu'il regarde, c'est celle-là que tu as à faire
>   afin de la lui donner.
> ...
> Une Prouhèze pour toujours que ne détruit pas la mort.[51]

I have drawn my example from only three plays, but there are many others. In the second version of *Partage de Midi*, revised to fit within the Christian framework, Ysé explains to Mésa that her function has been to "open" him, that the gift of self he had earlier offered to God had been "quelque chose de si serré que j'aurai bien voulu savoir comment il s'y serait pris pour l'ouvrir, le bon Dieu!"[52] In the same way, Beatrice tells Dante that the hurt she has done him was essential for his salvation, and begs his pardon:

> Il n'y avait vraiment pas d'autre moyen que de te rompre
>   pour t'ouvrir.
> Pour que le ciel avec la terre entre en toi, pour que Dieu
>   **pénètre**,
> Pardonne qu'une autre main n'aurait su approfondir
> La blessure que j'avais faite.[53]

---

[50] *Le Soulier de Satin*, II, p. 1056.
[51] Ibid., p. 1057.
[52] *Partage de Midi*, p. 52.
[53] *Feuilles de Saints*, "Ode Jubilaire," p. 684.

Claudel's insistence on the need for an opening is very similar to an attitude we encountered earlier in Péguy, although again the two poets arrive at a like conclusion by different paths. Péguy had compared the soul of what he termed "un honnête homme" to an imporous substance, sealed, as it were, with varnish. Only when an opening — also referred to as a "wound" — had been made could Grace enter. This occured at that moment when an individual realized the full anguish of the human condition, his own dependency and fragility.

Claudel frequently employs the word "intact" to express the idea of imporosity.* The cause of the "wound" — rejection by the loved one — is more specific and limited than Péguy's. Yet both come to the same thing: Prouhèze's role, explained by the angel, was to make Rodrigue understand "la dépendance, la nécessité et le besoin...," and human anguish is indeed summed up in the impossibility of achieving completion (perfection) in this world.

Taken at face value, Claudel's treatment of love would seem to fit within a Christian framework. Human love must ever remain imperfect, incomplete and may, moreover, divert man from his search for that which is complete and eternal. As St. Thomas observed, "It is not possible for any created good to constitute man's happiness... Hence it is evident that nought can lull man's will save universal good. This is not to be found in any creature but God alone." (*Summa theologica*, I-II, 2.8.) Violaine, Prouhèze, and to a lesser degree Claudel's other heroines, serve not as an end in themselves, but as a means, playing for their lovers the role of Beatrice for Dante. It is not accidental that Jacques almost repeats Dante's, "Beatrice in suso, ed io in lei guardava," (I gazed on Beatrice and she on high — Paradiso II, vs. 22) with his "Car ne sachant encore ce que je ferais, j'ai regardé où tu fixais le noir des yeux."[54] Despite Claudel's denial of Dante's influence, the similarity is obvious and has been pointed out by several critics. In both cases, as Anthony Viscuisi observes, "The poet perceives in exterior real-

---

* For example, Pierre calls Violaine "un être intact et neuf" (I, p. 573) at the moment it seems her future with Jacques is assured. See also the later discussion in this chapter of Sygne's question, "Mais à quoi sert d'être intact? Le grain que l'on met dans la terre / De quel usage est-il, s'il ne pourrit d'abord?" (Tome II, p. 285).

[54] *L'Annonce*, II, p. 113.

ity, in the eyes of Beatrice, the mystery of his soul and existence, but also the solution of the mystery and the point of departure for a journey to the Love that animates the material world." [55]

Yet there is a subtle and very important difference between Claudel's idea of love and that of Dante. Whereas Beatrice disappears, that is, she is absorbed in the general radiance of the final vision,* both Violaine and Prouhèze hold out the specific promise of personal reunion in heaven. Violaine pledges: "Et alors quand ce sera ton tour et que tu verras la grande porte craquer et remuer, c'est moi de l'autre côté qui suis après," [56] and Prouhèze knows that when she will have achieved Rodrigue's salvation by opening in him "ce vide impitoyable," she will have won him as her eternal husband: "C'est alors que je le donnerai à Dieu découvert et déchiré pour qu'il remplisse dans un coup de tonnere, *c'est alors que j'aurai un époux et que je tiendrai un dieu entre mes bras!*" [57] ** [italics added]. There is, in fact, a glorification of love as an absolute value which is not Christian at all, but rather owes more to the medieval concept of courtly love. Ernest Beaumont, in an excellent study of the Beatrice motif in Claudel, raises this point. In the 1898 version of *La Jeune Fille Violaine,* Violaine had clearly stated that the marriage bond between Mara and Jacques is stronger than any which could exist between herself and Jacques,[58] but in the 1911 version she becomes, not merely the "soul-mother" of Aubaine, but in a certain fashion, her mother in flesh and blood. She herself explains this to Jacques, "Ah, ne dis pas que je ne connais rien de toi! / Ni que j'ignore l'effort et la division de la femme

---

[55] Anthony Viscuisi, "Order and Passion in Claudel and Dante," *French Review,* XXX (March 6, 1967), p. 444.

* Dante exclaims: "And so my love to Him was wholly plighted / That Beatrice was in eclipse forgot / Nor this displeased her." (*Paradiso* X, vs. 56-58).

[56] *L'Annonce,* II, p. 94.

[57] *Le Soulier de Satin,* II, p. 1039.

** There is evidence that Claudel himself was somewhat troubled and unclear in his own thinking. For example, after the guardian angel promises Prouhèze will be reunited with Rodrigue in heaven in her incorruptible form Prouhèze asks, "Je serai à lui pour toujours dans mon âme et dans mon corps?" the angel's answer is equivocal: "Il nous faut laisser le corps en arrière quelque peu."

[58] *Violaine,* I, p. 630.

qui donne la vie!"⁵⁹ As Beaumont points out, Claudel is here disassociating marriage and human love and "making of the latter something peculiarly transcendent, even to the extent of causing a resurrected child's eyes to change color and resemble those of the father's soul-lover instead of the mother's eyes, and of conferring on the soul-lover a temporary supply of milk which establishes a further bond between her and the child conceived by her sister."⁶⁰ In a virulent critique of *L'Annonce,* the Catholic writer Francois Ducaud-Bourget castigates Claudel on this issue, claiming that the insistance on the mystery of the incarnation in a scene "si particulièrement et subtilement charnelle" is nothing but camouflaged blasphemy.⁶¹

Moreover, even though Prouhèze and Violaine are Claudel's "purest" creations, *love occurs outside of marriage.* As a matter of fact, marriage in Claudel's work is almost downgraded. In *La Maison fermée,* where he speaks of his wife as his "guardian" there is no mention of what we think of as romantic love. And see how Sichel describes her marriage to Louis: "Tu sais qu'entre ton père et moi, tu peux appeler cela un mariage, oui, ce fut une espèce d'alliance réfléchie. / Un pacte politique."⁶² Mara, referring to her union with Jacques, graphically depicts her despair: "Il naît de la douleur! Cet amour ne naît point de la joie, mais il naît de la douleur! cette douleur qui est la même chose que notre vie!"⁶³ Even the Pope draws a rather dismal picture. When Orian speaks of his love for Pensée the Pope chides him:

Dans tout ce que vous dites je ne vois que la passion et
    les sens et aucun esprit de prudence et de crainte de Dieu.
Cette jeune fille vous a plu et vous ne voyez rien d'autre,
Mais le mariage n'est point le plaisir, c'est le sacrifice
    du plaisir, c'est l'étude de deux âmes qui pour toujours
    désormais et pour une fin hors d'elles-mêmes
Auront à se contenter l'une de l'autre.⁶⁴

---

⁵⁹ *L'Annonce,* II, p. 92.
⁶⁰ Ernest Beaumont, *The Theme of Beatrice in the Plays of Claudel* (London: Rockliff, 1954), p. 29.
⁶¹ François Ducard-Bourget, et al., *Claudel, Mauriac et C*ⁱᵉ (Paris: Ed. de l'Ermite, 1951), p. 32.
⁶² *Le Père humilié,* II, p. 487.
⁶³ *Violaine,* I, p. 641.
⁶⁴ *Le Père humilié,* II, p. 523.

Monsieur Badilon's description of the married state is hardly calculated to attract Sygne to an alliance with Turelure, whom she already detests:

> ... Prenez-garde et faites attention à ce grand sacrement
> qu'est le mariage, de crainte qu'il ne soit profané.
> Ce que Dieu a crée, Il le consomme en nous. Il achève
> le pain et le vin.
> Il consomme l'huile. Il donne effet pour l'éternité à
> cette parole qu'Il nous a communiquée. Il fait un
> sacrement comme Son Corps même
> De cet aveu par qui le pécheur se condamne à mort.
> Ah, comme le corps d'un prêtre frémit, quand ce monstre
> qui est le frère de Jésus tournant vers lui sa face
> décomposée avoue par l'orifice de son corps pourri! [65]

It would seem, in fact, that love in the passionate, romantic sense — which Claudel is so adept at portraying elsewhere — has no place in marriage. "Ce n'est pas l'amour qui fait le mariage mais le consentement ... le consentement en présence de Dieu dans la foi," [66] Pélage observes.

It is possible that Claudel admired Dante precisely because Dante was able to cast the tradition of courtly love (and his adoration for Beatrice *is* in that tradition) into a wholly Christian framework. In the first place, Dante had loved Beatrice only at a distance in her lifetime; her death precluded any more intimate relationship. Thus, his love was, perforce, purified. Moreover, as already noted, Beatrice, as an individual, is absorbed into the final heavenly vision. But, however much Claudel's heroes protest it is a "soul" they seek (and this particular phraseology appears often), their actions belie their words. Orian does possess Pensée; Mésa, Ysé. Pierre had tried, though without success, to assault Violaine. And Rodrigue, who continually talks of the transcendent nature of his love, contradicts himself in a moment of jealous rage: "Elle s'est donnée à ce Camille, pourquoi ne se donnerait-elle à moi? / Je me moque de son âme! C'est son corps qu'il me faut, pas autre chose que son corps, la scélérate complicité de son corps!" [67] Moreover, and paralleling the mystery of Violaine's motherhood, it is hinted — and

---

[65] *L'Otage,* II, p. 268.
[66] *Le Soulier de Satin,* II, p. 1000.
[67] Ibid., p. 1016.

Camille believes — that Rodrigue is actually the "soul-father" of Camille's daughter, and comes nightly in spirit to visit Prouhèze. He refers to Rodrigue as "Votre visiteur habituel sans doute et le père de mon enfant," and then asserts, "Mais je sais que lui seul est le père de cette fille que je vous ai faite et qui ne ressemble qu'à lui." [68] The young girl herself addresses Rodrigue in a letter as "papa."

Beaumont makes a psychologically valid point when he states that while Claudel's faith causes him to redeem human love and use it for the salvation of the lovers, "The obvious flaw in this conception is that while the human love is irresistible, predestined, its transmutation into divine love is the artifice of the poet, not the logical outcome of the initial action." [69] Nowhere is this clearer than in *Partage de Midi*, which is surely the most autobiographical of Claudel's plays, and which has been compared to a modern Tristan ballad. Here, scarcely veiled by religious motifs, we find in the first version a concept of love which is clearly *l'amour courtois*. That love will be almost forced — and in my opinion, to the detriment of the drama — into a Christian framework before the author would permit the play to be shown on the stage.

Look at a few of the motifs usually associated with *l'amour courtois*. There is the "blessure inguérissable" which only the loved one — here, Ysé — can cure. The love is outside of marriage. In fact, even when de Ciz dies and Ysé is free to marry Mésa, she betrays him for Almaric. The magic "recognition" or "call," * a tradition in the *roman courtois,* is stressed. "C'est moi, Ysé. Je suis Mésa, c'est moi!" [70] These words, almost without variation, appear on five separate occasions. Like Tristan and Isolde, both Mésa and Ysé sense that should they respond to the call, the results will be fatal. Ysé warns Mésa, "Si vous m'appelez par mon nom / ... Il y a une femme en moi qui ne pourra pas s'empêcher de vous répondre. / Et je sens que cette femme ne serait point bonne / Pour vous, mais funeste, et pour moi il s'agit de choses affreuses!" [71] as later he will tell her, "Je le lis enfin, et j'en ai horreur, dans tes

---

[68] Ibid., p. 1067.
[69] Beaumont, p. 95.
* For other examples of the "call" motif see *Le Soulier de Satin*, and *L'Histoire de Tobie et de Sara*.
[70] *Partage de Midi*, I, pp. 1003, 1007, 1008, 1044, 1055.
[71] Ibid., p. 1008.

yeux le grand appel panique!" [72] The two of them vow not to love one another, but as in the Tristan legend, their vow is countermanded by fate.

Most importantly, and here again in the tradition of *l'amour courtois,* the love between Mésa and Ysé becomes an absolute value unto itself, as is clear from the following:

> YSÉ: Et voilà le passé et l'avenir en même temps
> Renoncées, et il n'y a plus de famille, et d'enfants et de mari et d'amis
> Et tout l'univers autour de nous
> Vide de nous comme une chose incapable de comprendre et qui demande la raison!
> MÉSA: Il n'y pas de raison que toi-même.
> YSÉ: Moi, je comprends, mon bien aimé,
> Et je suis comprise, et je suis la raison entre tes bras, et je suis Ysé, ton âme! [73]

This sort of love is, in essence, a substitute for religion. In the "Cantique de Mésa" Claudel tries, but without honest success, to reconcile Mésa's aspirations toward God with his love for Ysé. Mésa compares his suffering to that of Christ on the cross, and is sure that God will understand and forgive: "Ah, Vous vous y connaissez, Vous savez, Vous, / Ce que c'est que l'amour trahi! Ah, je n'ai point peur de Vous./" [74] Yet, in the midst of this prayer these words stand out:

> Je l'aimais, et je n'ai point peur de Vous,
> Et au-dessus de l'amour
> Il n'y a rien, et pas Vous-même! [75]

As mentioned earlier, the ending of the play would be drastically revised by Claudel for the stage. The "Cantique de Mésa" is much changed — the three offending verses have been deleted — and Ysé is cast into a Beatrice-like role. But in the first version there can be no doubt: their love is a transcendent thing, alone responsible for their ultimate salvation. Death will bring with it transfiguration.

---

[72] Ibid., p. 1030.
[73] Ibid.
[74] Ibid., p. 1053.
[75] Ibid.

Then Ysé will be "la femme pleine de beauté déployée dans la beauté plus grande!" and Mésa, triumphant, "le grand mâle dans la gloire de Dieu, l'homme dans la splendeur de l'août, l'Esprit vainqueur dans la transfiguration de Midi!" [76]

In *Le Mythe de Tristan* Jacques Duron observes that if, in Claudel's theater and poetry, Beatrice wins, "... ce n'est pas que Tristan n'ait eu largement la parole." [77] It is interesting, from a psychological point of view, to examine the very evident struggle within the poet which he never entirely resolved. The Tristan myth has perhaps its most perfect expression in the music of Richard Wagner.* As a young man, Claudel admired Wagner inordinately. As an older man, he detested him just as passionately, and reserved for him some of his bitterest castigations. In the same way, he utterly rejected the romantic concept of love embodied in *l'amour courtois*:

> Combien les fumées romantiques de l'amour purement charnel et les braiements de ce grand âne de Tristan me paraissent ridicules! L'amour humain n'a de beauté que quand il n'est pas accompagné par la satisfaction... Quant aux voluptés de l'amour satisfait, aucun écrivain ne les a jamais dépeintes, car elles n'existent pas. Le paradis qui consisterait dans la possession totale d'une femme et dans la prise comme fin suprême de ce corps et de cette âme ne me semble en rien différer de l'enfer. [78]

Yet it is this kind of love which, knowingly or not, he has enshrined in his works!

The fascinating aspect about Claudel's handling of love lies in this paradox: while in legend Tristan and Isolde's guilty love brings about their own ruin, as well as the first taint to Arthur's court, and while Guenevere's adultery with Lancelot precipitates the failure of Arthur's noble — and Christian — experiment, the guilt of Ysé, Mésa, Rodrigue, Prouhèze *operates toward their salvation*. Dona Prouhèze herself finds this hard to believe: "L'amour hors du sacre-

---

[76] Ibid., p. 1064.
[77] Jacques Duron, p. 552.
* One might even wonder if Claudel quite unconsciously chose the name, Almaric (which he had seen on the sign of an umbrella shop!), because of its close phonetic similarity to Wagner's Alberic of the ring cycle.
[78] *Correspondance*, Jacques Rivière (Paris: Plon, 1926), p. 262.

ment n'est-il pas le péché?" and the angel's answer would seem to be Claudel's own: "Même le péché! Le péché aussi sert." [79]

Perhaps Claudel's quite unusual attitude toward human love can best be explained in terms of his personal experience and his faith in the utter goodness of God. Evil may indeed be "un élément créateur incontestable," but "Le Mal est ce qui n'est pas."

There is a final motif I should like to examine that is related to, or more properly, occurs simultaneously with suffering and sacrifice of human love, and it is what I will call, for lack of a better term, the *thème de semences*. Over and again we find words like *semences, grain, cellule, semailles, fécondité, œuf*. In *L'Otage*, for example, Sygne, having long ago made her own sacrifice of feudal honor and love, pleads with Georges to do likewise:

SYGNE: Viens avec moi où il n'y a plus de douleur.
GEORGES: Et plus d'honneur?
SYGNE: Plus de nom et aucun honneur.
GEORGES: Le mien est intact.
SYGNE: Mais à quoi sert d'être intact? Le grain que l'on met dans la terre,
              De quel usage est-il, s'il ne pourrit d'abord? [80]

In the *Maison fermée* the poet would not only be a sower — of churches, of God's measure — but himself "Comme une petite graine dont on ne sait ce que c'est / Et qui jetée dans une bonne terre en recueille toutes les énergies et produit une plante specifiée/," [81] for, as he asks, how can God enter our hearts of there is no home for him there: "Point de Dieu pour toi sans une église et toute vie commence par la cellule." [82] Nowhere does this image occur more frequently than in the various versions of *Violaine* and *L'Annonce*.

Now, before the seed can be implanted, the wound or opening must be made. Violaine does this for Pierre, and he becomes, as the poet of *La Maison fermée*, a "carrier," a sower of churches:

    Ne dites pas que je suis maçon, mais comme vous je suis
        un semeur de semences.

---

[79] *Le Soulier de Satin*, II, p. 1056.
[80] *L'Otage*, II, p. 285.
[81] *La Maison fermée*, p. 283.
[82] Ibid.

> Dans le milieu de la ville, dans le grouillant sol humain
> j'ai planté cette église comme une graine,
> Le germe inextinguible et la coque du vide seminal. [83]

Justitia, the martyr, becomes the inspiration for his church, and Pierre leaves her little milk teeth "comme une semence sous le grand bloc de base," [84] just as he will make of Violaine's sacrified wedding ring "une semence d'or." [85] Later, when Jacques asks him to return the ring, he replies, "Je ne le peux plus! Pas plus que l'épi complet ne peut rendre / Le grain dans la terre d'où sort sa tige." [86] The same seed-plant metaphor is used when he described the statue of Violaine which will crown his church: "Et je la représenterai les mains croisées sur la poitrine, comme l'épi encore à demi-prisonnier de ses téguments..." [87] In the final stage version, where Pierre no longer appears, the image is taken up by Anne:

> Ce n'est plus le temps de la moisson, c'est celui des semailles.
> La terre assez longtemps nous a nourris, et moi, il est temps
> que je la nourrisse à mon tour
>   *se retournant vers Violaine*
> De ce grain inestimable. [88]

Over and again I have had occasion to use words like "coïncidence," "imitation," "superposition." In the *semence* theme we have such an instance. Just as the sacrifice of Christ was the germ or seed from which grew the Church Eternal, so the martyrdom of Justitia, the suffering and death of Violaine are the seeds from which grew Pierre's church. Pierre draws the parallel: "Et nul s'il ne sort de grain ne sera de l'épi. / Et certes Justice est belle. Mais combien plus beau / Cet arbre fructifiant de tous les hommes que la semence eucharistique engendre en sa végétation." [89]

This *thème de semences* is, I feel, of central importance in Claudel's symbolism, and surprisingly, of medieval origin. But to show

---

[83] *Violante*, I, p. 653.
[84] *L'Annonce*, II, p. 18.
[85] Ibid., p. 25.
[86] Ibid., p. 106.
[87] Ibid., p. 108.
[88] Ibid., p. 209.
[89] Ibid., p. 109.

this, I must first refer back to the time structure discussed in Chapter II, as well as to Claudel's concept of space.

In that chapter I pointed out that Claudel's time structure was, like liturgical time, circular in nature. In this chapter we have so far considered only isolated attitudes or values which are essentially medieval, and for which Claudel felt a great affinity. But there is a subtler and far more profound reason for the attraction the poet felt for the Middle Ages. "Une loi, une foi, un roi," simplistically sums up the spirit of an era when people felt they were living in a *closed world*. It is precisely this closed world which Claudel is re-creating in his works. In *Le Repos du septième Jour* the Prime Minister describes the Emperor's empire in words which might well be applied to Claudel's own:

> A l'Ouest la Terre s'élève vers l'adoration;
> Le Nord borne ton empire, et les Rois du Sud
> Ont reçu ton sceau et t'envoient des tributs;
> Et à l'Est la mer
> Pacifique, sans borne, éternelle;
> De ce côté la porte noire du Ciel par où le Soleil apparaît.
> Telles sont les bornes de ton Empire.
> Et il est appelé l'Empire du Milieu, le Royaume-de-la-Tranquillité-du-Matin
> Il est rond comme une coupe... [90]

It is no accident that the importance of the closure is mentioned many times in Claudel's voluminous correspondence with Gide. On the subject of Coventry Patmore, whom he admired, Claudel wrote: "Lui aussi est un précurseur de cette doctrine qui, je le crois, sera celle du xxe siecle, la doctrine de la fermeture, de la fin, de l'inépuisable dans l'Eternellement formé." [91] Or again, in a discussion regarding Bergson, he stresses the necessity of what he calls "un vase clos" [92] and continues, "C'est l'idée de *forme* ou de *fermeture* à laquelle j'attache de plus en plus d'importance." [93] Also in his letters to Gide he would reproch the Hindu poet, Tagore, for not having, as he put it, a "center."

---

[90] *Le Repos du Septième Jour*, I, p. 798.
[91] *Correspondance*, Claudel, Gide, p. 125.
[92] Ibid., p. 106.
[93] Ibid.

That Claudel was consciously recreating in his poetry a closed world is very clearly stated in another letter to Gide, earlier quoted, in which he writes of the themes of *Art poetique* and the *Odes*: "L'inépuisable dans le fermeture, le cercle qui est le type de toute forme, fini et cependant infini, œuf, semence, bouche ouverte, zéro ..." [94]

Now, this circle exists in both time and space, a fact brought out both by Andre Vachon in his book, *Le Temps et l'Espace dans l'Œuvre de Paul Claudel* and by Georges Poulet in *Hommage à Paul Claudel*. As Claudel himself explains in *Art poétique, co-naissance* may be thought of as having the form of vibrations which go out in concentric waves from the self to that which is non-self, knowledge of the non-self being obtained through the resistance which the waves encounter. There is, however, a boundless desire in Claudel to expand and possess all that is non-self. This expansion held grave dangers. As Poulet points out:

> Un des périls littéraires auxquels le XX° siecle a échappé est le spectacle d'un Claudel de plus en plus volumineux, obstruant les espaces imaginaires. Devant lui il aurait fait le vide, en lui aurait fait le plein, et cela à perte de vue; de sorte qu'en fin de compte il n'y aurait plus eu dans l'univers qu'un Claudel énorme, sphérique, qui, comme Léviathan, aurait "possédé la mer éternelle." [95]

This, of course, was the danger inherent in Tête d'Or. With his conversion, with God, Claudel discovered his boundaries. Writes Poulet: "Il touche son terme. Il se reconnaît en deçà de l'infini. Dès lors l'espace où il s'enflait circulairement change de caractère. C'est l'espace fini, qu'entoure, comme au moyen âge, un espace infini, Dieu où l'Empyrée." [96] Poulet also remarked the circular nature of Claudel's time, comparing it aptly to an enormous clock dial, on which the hour is told not by a moving hand, but by the circular movement of the dial, so that it is, as Claudel maintained, all hours at any hour. [97]

---

[94] Ibid., p. 91.
[95] Georges Poulet, "Œuf, Semence, Bouche ouverte, Zéro," *Hommage à Paul Claudel*, p. 452.
[96] Ibid., p. 453.
[97] Ibid., p. 458.

Earlier I had said that Claudel's life work is, in effect, a cathedral. Here I have spoken of a closed, circular world. That these two concepts are in no way contradictory is clear from "Le Développement de l'Eglise," where Claudel discusses the fundamental need in man for closure. In fact, as we shall see, there are both *object-symbols* in his work and a circular *movement*. Movement and symbols are intended to convey the same basic idea. Poulet expresses this very clearly:

> De même que pour Dante et Denys l'Aréopagite, l'église souffrante comme l'Eglise triomphante sont pour Claudel une disposition et un mouvement autour du centre, une orientation vers lui. De tous côtés vers cette réalité centrale l'univers fait pente... La création est une Eglise, et cette église, comme celle de Pierre de Craon, est disposée de telle sorte que "de tous les points dans des cadres sans cesse changeants, on ne cesse point d'envisager le Centre sacré dans les Flammes." Autour du centre la création fait cercle.[98]

Now, a familiar medieval representation of the world was an enormous circle with Christ within. But that closed universe was shattered, as Carl Gustav Jung observed, by the Reformation and the Renaissance. In his well-documented study, *Psychology and Religion,* Jung writes: "... modern man, Protestant or not, has lost the protection of the ecclesiastical walls carefully erected and reinforced since Roman days, and on account of that loss has approached the zone of world-destroying and world-creating fire. Our world is permeated by waves of restlessness and fear."[99]

Jung became intrigued by a certain type of dream which he encountered among his patients. One, for example, involved what the patient described as "a solemn house of inner composure," another, a giant clock face. In these and similar dreams the dreamer invariably experienced a sense of "most sublime harmony." In *Psychology and Religion,* Jung retraces his thinking, which led him into research into the importance — particularly in the Middle Ages — of the circle. He found in the work of an obscure medieval poet, Guil-

---

[98] Ibid., p. 465.
[99] Carl Gustav Jung, *Psychology and Religion,* tr. R. F. C. Hull (New Haven, Conn.: Yale University Press, 1968), p. 59.

laume de Digulleville, a vision of paradise as a great golden orb, around which rolled a tiny azure blue circle. An angel explained to him that the circle was the calendar — the liturgical calendar — but of eternity, not ordinary time. This reminded Jung of various medieval representations of the world, always either circular or approximating a circle: the *melothesiae,* where the horizon was formed by the zodiac, the *rex gloriae,* with the triumphant Christ surrounded by the four evangelists. Various symbols associated with Mary, the *vas devotionis,* the *rosa mystica,* the *hortus conclusus* were also circular in form. He noted that there were Eastern analogies: mandalas approximating the circle, such as a lotus with a four-sided building within it, and in the center, a Buddha or Shiva.

To Jung, all of these things symbolized, in a more or less obvious way, a closed world with a *God within.* Modern man, shorn of the protection of such a world, desperately sought after a new security, and a new God within. This theory accounted for the extraordinary sense of peace, harmony, etc., experienced by the dreamers mentioned above.

I am not in any way trying to apply Jungian psychoanalytics to Claudel. In fact, Claudel would have represented an anomaly to Jung, for he did indeed find a God, whereas Jung contends that modern man finally finds himself, Man, where God once stood. Nevertheless, his argument as to the naturalness of the "O" symbol seems quite convincing. It became even more so, as regards Claudel, when Jung goes on to point out the variations which the circle may take: flowers (and particularly the rose!), a clock, a cross, a church, a filled bowl or vase, a ring, an egg or seed — precisely those which occur with greatest frequency in Claudel. *

Columbus is admired because he circumnavigates the earth, proving that it is, in fact, a *globe.* I mentioned earlier the privileged place of the letter "O." ** "O," writes Claudel, "C'est le miroir,

---

* As a matter of fact, one of the circular symbols to which Jung alludes, the *Hortus Conclusus,* which refers to the closed garden in the *Song of Songs* and was identified first with the Church, then the Virgin, is the title and subject of one of Claudel's later (1941) and very obscure poems in which both the Virgin and the rose appear (v. *Œuvre poetique,* p. 882).

** Rousseau tells in his *Confessions* the story of an old woman who repeated "O" as her only prayer. Her wise confessor understood, and told her, "Bonne mère, continuez de prier toujours ainsi; votre prière vaut mieux que les nôtres." (v. Pléiade édition of *Œuvres complètes,* I, Livre XII, p. 642).

William T. Starr of Northwestern University suggests that the Zen "Om"

à moins que ce ne soit le vide parfait et le rond de l'âme dilatée vers l'esprit oral." [100] By the same token, the *bouche ouverte* is (in French, the *oui*) the circular symbol of consent: that is why Anne insists on Elizabeth's verbal permission: "Dis oui, Elizabeth ... Le oui qui nous sépare, à cette heure, bien bas, aussi plein que celui qui nous a faits jadis un seul." [101] The marriage ring is just another form of the *bouche ouverte*. Anne refers to it as "l'Anneau qui a la forme d'un oui." [102] Jung had mentioned the cross. Obviously this is an important symbol in Claudel. Both Rodrigue's brother, the Jesuit priest, and the Princess of *Tête d'Or* are crucified. But notice in the following the circularity attributed to the Cross. Anne sets off to see the hole that the cross made when it was planted in the ground, telling Elizabeth:

> La voici qui tire tout à elle
> Là est le point qui ne peut être défait, le nœud qui ne
>   peut être dissous,
> Le patrimoine commun, la borne intérieure qui ne peut être
>   arrachée
> Le centre et l'ombilic de la terre, le milieu de l'humanité
>   qui tout tient ensemble. [103]

The Emperor in *Le Repos du septième Jour* returns from his visit to the other world, carrying a new scepter which has the form of a cross, and he tells his people:

> Regardez tous! voici ce que je rapporte! Je tiens entre
>   mes mains le signe royal et salutaire!
> Voici la sublime intersection en qui le ciel est joint à
>   la terre par l'homme.
> Voici le jugement entre la droite et la gauche, la sépa-
>   ration du haut et du bas, voici l'oblation et le sacrifice!
> Voici le très-saint Milieu, le centre d'où s'ecartent
>   également les quatre lignes, voici l'ineffable point.
> Considère ce signe, ô monde! [104]

---

is a similar expression of human awe in the face of the wonder and harmony of creation.

[100] Œuvres complètes, XX, *L'Epée et le Miroir*, p. 43.
[101] *L'Annonce*, II, p. 32.
[102] *Violaine*, I, p. 581.
[103] *L'Annonce*, II, p. 32.
[104] *Le Repos du Septième Jour*, I, p. 844.

It is as if the four lines of the cross pulled all space around them to form a circle of which the cross itself is the center.

There is nothing at all haphazard about Claudel's symbolism. I have already mentioned the "empty cup" symbol which Anne used. Violaine, looking forward to her marriage with Jacques, is told by Pierre, "Ainsi votre coupe est pleine. Que pourriez-vous attendre ou recevoir?" [105] Yet this is not true, for her cup is not full. The necessary *vide* exists; she thirsts, and can only be filled by the spiritual source. It is fascinating to see the final transformation of the circle symbol: it is the *semence, œuf, grain,* true, but Claudel goes one step further. It is the Living Word. Violaine dimly understands this when she tells Pierre, "Parlez, car je vous écoute." He responds:

La parole, jeune fille,
Ne se forme point comme une note sous le doigt de l'organiste
    quand le pied presse le soufflet.
Mais longuement, obscurément,
Plus profond que le cœur et les intestins, pendant le
    repas et la marche, pendant les silencieuses heures de
    travail, elle se constitue
Comme un œuf spirituel en nous, comme la capsule séminale . . . [106]
[italics added]

Most significantly, this conversation takes place at the privileged hour of midnight, "entre l'heure de la lune et celle du soleil . . . et l'on ne sait si c'est hier ou demain." [107] It is at this magic moment that Pierre would make his gift to Violaine:

O Violaine! Oubliez à ce moment, comme je les oublie
Hier, demain, et comme un être intact et neuf, recueillie
    tout entière sur l'heure présente
Acceuillez cette parole inconnue dont je sens en moi le
    travail et la poussée. [108] [italics added]

Here we have a coming together of the various themes and symbols already discussed — the word identified with *un œuf spirituel,* the moment of fertilization being the Present, which partakes

---

[105] *Violaine,* I, p. 573.
[106] Ibid.
[107] Ibid.
[108] Ibid.

of neither past nor future. Pierre goes on to talk of the spiritual source (the *fons signatus,* another Mary symbol, found in Claudel's favorite *Cantique des Cantiques*). Violaine, retaining the vase image, asks, "Qui éprouverait la mesure du vase / Autrement qu'en le remplissant?" Pierre answers, "Il est des gens, O Violaine, ... a qui nulle abondance ne suffit, s'ils ne boivent à la vive source eux-mêmes, y appliquant la bouche." It is at this point that Violaine exclaims, "Hélas, parole irréparable!" [109]

I had said there was a circular *movement* as well as various circle object-symbols. Here Violaine and Pierre are acting out the intellectualized statement quoted above, "O, c'est le miroir, à moins que ce ne soit le vide parfait et le rond de l'âme dilatée vers l'esprit oral." Violaine, thirsting, receives the word which will fill her, dilate her soul in a round imitation of the Virgin. Like Mary she will reply, "Behold the handmaid of the Lord," and like her, she will "conceive." When Mara repeats the third verse of the Angelus — *Et le verbe s'est fait chair et il a habité parmi nous* — she refers, not only to Christ, but to Violaine's child, Aubaine, "Cet enfant à moi que j'ai enfanté et c'est elle qui l'a mis au monde." [110]

First there must be the opening, then the thirst, then the implantation of the seed, and finally the suffering which often ends in physical death precisely because the vase, vial, or what-have-you must be crushed so that the seed can be released and replanted. In French this makes a very nice alliterative circle, or rather, near circle:

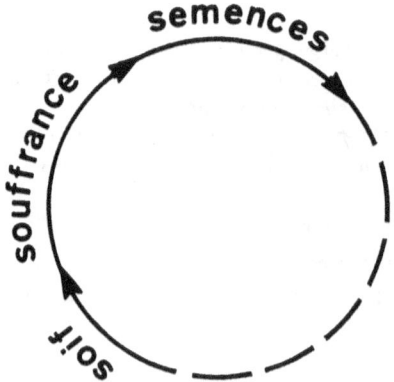

---

[109] Ibid., p. 578.
[110] *L'Annonce,* II, p. 210.

This, and nothing else, is what the Princess means when she cries, "Oh! puissé-je être comme la fleur coupée dont le parfum est plus fort," [111] or Violaine, when she says, "Maintenant je suis rompue toute entière, et le parfums exhale." [112] Although the circle is not completed in any play, the direction of movement is clearly indicated. Almost all of Claudel's plays end on a note of renewal, indicating that the whole thing will begin again at some other time, in some other place. *La Ville* significantly ends on Easter. Orian dies, but Pensée carries his child within her. Rodrigue is defeated, but in defeat hears the cannons which announce the triumphal marriage of his "daughter." As Anne, filled with joy, realizes, "A la fleur succède le fruit qu'on mange, et au fruit / De nouveau les fleurs!" [113]

All of this is not to deny that Violaine's hour is not her particular hour. It is, in the sense of her individual death. But it is also all hours at once. That is why significant events occur at those times when there is no time, as Pierre and Violaine's conversation, Aubaine's rebirth at midnight, Christmas, Violaine's death at the autumn solstice. *La Cantate à trois Vois* in like manner takes place at the spring solstice, and at an hour "quand le matin est une seule chose avec le soir." [114] Claudel wrote of this work, "C'est la nuit où le soleil s'arrête, où la nature parvenue en son plein épanouissement demeure en un suspens solennel... Tout passe, il est vrai, mais pour revenir chaque année au même point d'extase. La fleur passe, mais non point le délice qui émane d'elle." [115] The solstice, midnight, noon, these are privileged moments because the instant "qui se sépare en deux laisse par un étroit interstice filtrer l'éternité." [116] The Eternal hour is thus superposed on the terrestrial hour. Before Violaine was Joan, and before Joan, Justitia, and others will come in future years to follow their example. As Claudel wrote to Jacques Rivière, "La véritable image de l'infini est le cercle, le zéro... Or le cercle est en même temps la parfaite image du fini, de la création réalisée." [117]

---

[111] *Tête d'Or*, I, p. 158.
[112] *L'Annonce*, II, p. 89.
[113] *L'Annonce*, II, p. 100.
[114] *La Cantate à Trois Voix*, p. 327.
[115] *Œuvre poétique*, "Notes," p. 1086.
[116] Ibid., p. 1089.
[117] *Correspondance*, Rivière, p. 61.

This is also what he meant when he said that he wished to reproduce in *Corona Benignitatis Anni Dei* "l'immuable itinéraire dont le Christ a fixé les étapes." His characters — his saints — do nothing more than follow this immutable itinerary within the theater he has constructed for them.

In *Art Poétique* Claudel had posed for himself the two essential questions: "Je suis, mais je suis où? Quelle heure donc est-il, en moi et hors de moi?"[118] His entire poetic output is an attempt to answer those questions. He is the astronomer who, in "La Lampe et la Cloche" contemplates, "les yeux sur le cadran le plus complet, l'heure totale."[119]

> L'heure sonne, de par l'action de l'immense ciel illuminé! De la pendule enfouie au cœur d'une chambre de malade au grand Ange flamboyant qui dans le Ciel successivement gagne tous les points prescrits à son vol circulaire, il y a une exacte réponse. Je ne sers pas à computer une autre heure. Je ne l'accuse pas avec une moindre décision.[120]

The hour of Claudel is indisputably the Present, of which he is eternally a part. Into that Present he would re-install, as it were, the *essential* values which he felt existed during the Middle Ages, and which must, because they are essential, still exist. Among these, as we have seen, were the vast rite of the Church, with its splendid, reiterative ceremony, and an other-world orientation which explains, indeed necessitates suffering and renunciation in this world.

Woman would have a central role in this re-installation, though, as I have indicated, and contrary to Claudel's stated intention, she is not simply the Soul, the Church, the Virgin, or Wisdom. She is *anima* in a more general sense, the feminine element, Goethe's *das Ewig-Weibliche,* Eve, the temptress, as well as Mary, Mother of God. Here Claudel drew sustenance, perhaps unconsciously, from the ancient tradition of *l'amour courtois,* and then, by curious means, fit this concept into the Christian concept.

I have tried to show that the poetic and philosophic structure which Claudel erected is a duplication of the closed universe of the

---

[118] *Art poétique,* p. 141.
[119] *Connaissance de l'est,* p. 109.
[120] Ibid.

Middle Ages; that there is a sweeping identification between that universe and the Church Eternal, manifested through the office, the liturgical year, and a variety of symbols, many originally medieval, all involving closure, and the most perfect being the circle.

Moreover, Claudel's "imitation," through the poet's word — itself a repetition of the Word — involves not only natural or traditional symbols, but a cyclical movement in action and content, and finally, in the poet's own life. It is no accident that he chose for the inscription of his tomb: *Ici reposent les restes et les semences de Paul Claudel.*

What he had written so long ago to Gide in reference to the *Odes* applies to his entire work: "Ce que peindront mes Odes, c'est la joie d'un homme que le silence des espaces n'effraie plus." Space was no longer limitless, Pascal's abyss had been closed. Through his poetry, and in a very present context, Claudel had rebuilt the walls that once enclosed *une foi, une loi, un roi.* In the exact center and at the outermost extremity is God.

Chapter V

RE-PRESENTATION

> Car il y a dans l'enfant, car il y a dans l'enfance une grâce unique. Une entièreté, une premièreté Totale.
> *Le Mystère des Saints innocents*

We have seen what the Middle Ages represented for Claudel. But what did Péguy intend to convey, in terms of time and values, by his persistent use of the expression, *ancienne France?*

The first part of the proposition — what was *ancienne France* in terms of a specific period — is extraordinarily difficult to resolve, precisely because of Péguy's notion of time and of history. He had stated, "Le bergsonisme n'est point une géographie, c'est une géologie."[1] He insisted on a sort of archeological excavation in time. The problem in limiting any particular period lies in the fact that, according to the theory of interpenetration of moments, no one period ends abruptly. As Clio explains, "Je ne peux pas conter une histoire, on ne voit jamais le commencement de mes histoires premièrement parce que toute histoire n'est pas limitée, parce que toute histoire est tissue dans l'histoire infinie, deuxièmement parce que, dans leur système, toute histoire elle-même est infinie."[2] As earlier noted, the Christian city of which *ancienne France* is part did not spring up overnight, but was built slowly on the Hebrew and Greco-Roman cities which preceded it, all of which form part of modern man's heritage.

---

[1] "Note sur M. Bergson," II, p. 1314.
[2] "Clio," II, p. 242.

Just how closely Péguy identifies these three civilizations is apparent from the following:

> Au regard du temps moderne l'antique et le chrétien vont ensemble, sont ensemble: les deux antiques, l'hébreu, le grec. 'Le chrétien était autrefois un antique.' Jusqu'en 1880. Il faut aujourd'hui qu'il soit un moderne.[3]

Or again, in his essay on Descartes:

> Je l'ai dit vingt fois: la lutte (et une lutte mortelle), le débat, la lutte n'est pas entre le monde chrétien et le monde antique... La lutte est entre le monde moderne, d'une part, et d'autre part tous les autres mondes ensemble. Et notamment entre le monde moderne, d'une part, et d'autre part le monde antique et le monde chrétien ensemble.[4]

There is, then, no sharp break between the antiquities and *ancienne France*: "*Leurs sorts sont liés... C'est la spiritualité qui est poursuivie dans les uns et dans l'autre.*"[5] Yet, according to Péguy's concept of *vieillissement* cultures give birth to new cultures and themselves grow old and die. Even within longer periods, there are separate and distinct centuries, although these are not necessarily divided by an arbitrary hundred years. As Clio says, "... il y a des siècles, non seulement des siècles de comptage, de comptabilité horokilométrique, mais des siècles de l'évènement de l'histoire."[6] The eighteenth century, for example, begins with the death of Louis XIV and ends with the Revolution. In an analogous way, the Hebrew and Greco-Roman antiquities begin to die with the birth of Christ. As they die, Christianity begins to grow, and with it (or very shortly thereafter), *ancienne France*.

One may properly question why Péguy, who disliked fixing dates, should mark the beginning of *le monde moderne* clearly at 1880. The reason is simple: in that year the first of three laws was passed which, by 1882, would make secular public education compulsory in France. Under this educational system, Péguy would

---

[3] "Argent," II, p. 1129.
[4] "Note conjointe sur M. Descartes," II, p. 1533.
[5] Ibid.
[6] "Clio," II, p. 297.

maintain, children began to un-learn all that they had known naturally: those basic truths which man has ever known, from the beginning of time.

One can, then, set some sort of time limits around *ancienne France,* vague at one end, precise at the other. It is another, and even more difficult task to try to determine what this period represented in terms of values and attitudes. One cause of the difficulty lies in Péguy's basic approach. While Claudel's thought structure is intellectually very complex, it is still possible — precisely because it is an intellectual structure — to analyze and systematize it. Péguy resists systematization. Anyone writing about him must feel a little like poor Clio: could she but seize the truth by intuition, what a history she would write! As Yves Vadé observes in *Péguy et le Monde moderne,* Péguy showed little interest in such thinkers as Goethe, Hegel, or Nietzsche, or, in fact, in intellectual systems as such. "Il ne procède pas par totalisation après une vaste enquête, il ne cherche pas à élaborer une synthèse. Une telle démarche lui paraîtrait encore dangereusement intellectuelle." [7]

Moreover, in his effort to re-create and re-present, Péguy, in considering *ancienne France* as a source of renewal is really considering the *mystique* of *ancienne France.* He opposes the two words, *mystique* and *politique* so frequently that it would be well to define them. *Le mystique* is the idea in its pure form; *le politique,* the inevitable corruption of that idea in its application. Thus Christ and his teachings are *le mystique* of Christianity; the institution of the Church, *le politique.* To give another example, *le mystique* of the socialist revolution was for Péguy changed into *le politique* by the actions of men such as Jaurès, who compromised the purity of the revolutionary vision even as they sought to make that vision a reality.

In Péguy's works, *le mystique* of *ancienne France* is diametrically opposed to *le politique* of the modern world. To understand the former it might be helpful to try to define it, as the Hindus define Brahma, by negation. If *ancienne France* stands in opposition to *le monde moderne,* what, indeed, is the latter?

---

[7] Yves Vadé, *Péguy et le Monde moderne* (Quercy-Auverge: Amitié de Charles Péguy, 1965), p. 108.

First of all, modern, as Péguy uses it, is in nowise synonymous with contemporary, nor does it necessarily imply any chronological order (while Jeanne was of *ancienne France,* Charles VII was a "modern" king). *Le monde moderne* is, rather, a composite of attitudes and practices. Vadé observes:

> ... systèmes intellectuels et pratiques, politiques, sont liés comme toujours à un certain état de la civilisation, à certaines valeurs sociales, à une certaine société. Le culte de l'efficacité (qui s'oppose aux règles de l'honneur et, en politique, fonde le dogme de la raison d'état) le règne de la bourgeoisie et, par elle, le règne de l'argent, tels sont les principaux caractères de la société moderne.[8]

Henri-Victor Mallard, in *La Morale de Péguy,* offers the following definition: "Le monde moderne, c'est celui qui vit contrairement à la morale, dans l'habitude du péché, qui refuse la libération bergsonienne," and he adds, "Péguy n'est pas un homme du moyen âge, à moins que cela ne signifie qu'il est d'abord un homme de Dieu."[9]

In *La Tapisserie de sainte Geneviève* Péguy opposes the two systems: that of Christ, represented by *ancienne France,* and that of Satan, represented by *le monde moderne.* Just two stanzas suffice to show how far-reaching is this opposition:

> Les armes de Satan c'est notre quiétude
> Et c'est le théorème et c'est la certitude,
> Le pouvoir, le savoir et la décrépitude;
>
> Les armes de Jésus c'est notre inquiétude,
> L'axiome, la règle de notre incertitude,
> Le devoir, le pouvoir et la vicissitude.[10]

Again, we find Péguy opposing the complacency of modern man to the precarious position of the Christian. The arms of Satan are many other things, too: infidelity, dishonor, the seven cardinal sins, scientism, and most powerful of all, money:

---

[8] Ibid., p. 109.
[9] Henri Victor Mallard, *La Morale de Péguy* (Paris: Editions de l'Ermite, 1952), p. 109.
[10] *La Tapisserie de sainte Geneviève,* p. 859.

> Les armes de Satan c'est Jésus-Christ vendu,
> C'est les trente deniers, c'est Joseph descendu
> Au fond de la citerne et captif revendu. [11]

And, in summation, "Les armes de Satan c'est tout ce qui complique / La très simple existence." [12]

If, in seeking to set time limits to *ancienne France,* we saw the importance of the Bergsonian concept of interpenetration of moments, that concept is even more important in an attempt to determine the *values* which Péguy attributed to *ancienne France.* And here I should like to go back to an idea developed in Chapter III. There I had quoted a passage from *Le Mystère des Saints innocents,* reminiscent of Claudel, which referred to the closed, vaulted arch of God's world, temporal and eternal, of which the keystone is Christ. The stone preceding the keystone is the prophet, John the Baptist, and that immediately following it is Peter, apostle and saint. Péguy arrives at this final metaphor in a patient, laborious way, stressing throughout a long development the indissoluble union of carnal and spiritual, temporal and eternal, Old Testament and New. He recounts the long story of Joseph and his brothers, which he finds paralleled in the New Testament by the parable of the prodigal son: "Un homme avait douze fils..." and "Un homme avait deux fils..." But where Joseph is found again on a throne, the prodigal becomes a keeper of pigs. This, says Péguy, is typical of the difference between the two books. The Old Testament is directed toward command, government; the New, toward the misery of man; the Old concerns the kingdom of this world; the New, the eternal kingdom. "Ainsi marche le gouvernement des biens de ce monde / Avant le gouvernement des biens qui ne sont pas de ce monde. / Ainsi marche le commandement charnel / Avant le commendement spirituel." [13]

In one of the loveliest images to be found in his work, Péguy, by an "intuitive" metaphor, expresses the relationship between the Old Testament (and the Mosaic law) and the New Testament (Christianity).

---

[11] Ibid., p. 860.
[12] Ibid., p. 862.
[13] *Les Saints innocents,* p. 779.

Ou encore l'ancien testament est le lac profond qui reflète
  la haute forêt
Et la forêt est toute dans le lac mais elle n'y est pas.
Et le lac sombre et le lac profond est enfoncé dans la terre.
Et dans le lac le ciel est au fond.[14]

If this seems far afield from *ancienne France* it is not. In the "Note conjointe sur M. Descartes" Péguy writes at length of the Jewish race, which he calls the race of the *non-réussite*.* The Oriental fatalism which he attributes to the Jews finds its balance in Christianity in the spirit of revolt which he credits to the French. Both proceed from what he calls "un incurable souci." And it is through Jésus that this *souci* has been transmitted to the French people. "Et par Jésus la greffe incurable de ce souci sur les troncs plus durs de la force français. [sic] Ainsi est née la plus belle race de peine qui soit jamais venue au monde."[15] And that race constitutes *ancienne France*.

It is best here to let Péguy speak for himself, even though I must quote at some length.

> Pour obtenir une mélancolie de cette profondeur incurable, aussi creuse et aussi mortellement gravée il fallait cette greffe et ce sauvageon, il fallait cette race et il fallait cette autre race, il fallait cette âme et il fallait cette autre âme... il fallait un virus aussi antique introduit dans un corps jeune et sain et il faut le dire sans défense. Il fallait un virus aussi âcre et aussi sacré, macéré dans la seule race d'Orient qui eût été créée contre l'Orient, concentré par une reconcentration de trente et quarante siècles dans le secret de cette race, brusquement inséré dans une race neuve, dans tant d'innocence et tant de pureté, et dans cette tendresse, dans tant de nouveauté... dans une si belle force matérielle... il fallait l'opération de cette greffe unique inquiétude chrétienne et pour que la royale sagesse

---

[14] Ibid., p. 784.

* This is in no way a prejudicial epithet. Oddly enough, most of Péguy's closest friends were Jews: — Jules Isaac, Bernard Lazare, "le patron des *Cahiers*," Julien Benda; without its Jewish subscribers, according to Halévy, the *Cahiers* would have foundered. Péguy refers simply to the series of catastrophes, the last of which he was spared knowing, which have pursued God's "chosen people."

[15] "Note conjointe sur M. Descartes," II, p. 1368.

et la royale tristesse du roi Salonmon devînt la tragique et plus que royale détresse d'un Pascal.[16]

From the foregoing it should be clear that Péguy's concept of *ancienne France* comprehends all the assimilated values of the cultures which had gone before it: the purity of Greece, the grandeur of Rome, the Mosaic law as well as the new law contained in the Gospels. Yet Péguy speaks of France and only France. How can this apparent paradox be explained? His emphasis on the French "race," a word he uses freely, has even led some critics to accuse him of racism. Nothing could be more alien to his entire religious position.

His emphasis on France does, at first glace, seem far narrower than Claudel's comprehensive effort on behalf of the world. For Péguy, France has a "most favored nation" clause in its treaty with God. "Nos Français sont avancés entre tous. Ils sont mes témoins préférés."[17] True, God admits, "Mon fils m'a fait de très bons jardiniers,"[18] but of all his gardeners, none equal the French:

> Mais ici, dit Dieu, dans cette douce France, ma plus noble création,
> Dans cette saine Lorraine
> Ici ils sont bons jardiniers.
> C'est des vieux jardiniers finis, des fins jardiniers depuis
>   quatorze siècles qu'ils suivent les leçons de mon Fils.
> Ils ont tout canalisé, tout ameubli dans les jardins de l'âme.
> De l'eau qui sert à inonder, à empoisonner (*riant*) eux ils
>   s'en servent pour arroser.
> Peuple de mon Fils, peuple plein de grâce, éternellement
>   plein de jeunesse et de grâce.[19]

Despite the privileged position Péguy accords France, he is, in actuality, less exclusive than Claudel. For he, like his heroine, Jeanne, refuses to admit to the damnation of anyone, whereas for Claudel conversion — formal conversion to Roman Catholicism — seemed the unique road to salvation.* In his commentary on *Eve*,

---

[16] Ibid.
[17] *Le Porche*, p. 741.
[18] Ibid., p. 633.
[19] Ibid.

* Claudel's rather extravagant efforts to convert Gide finally provoked from the latter the beautiful response of *Le Retour de l'Enfant prodigue*.

Péguy points up the respect in which Jesus (and the poet) hold Eve and all her children. And he explains the bases for this respect: "On chercherait en vain dans les Evangiles trace d'un mépris quelconque: tout y est charité... ce qui revient à dire une fois de plus et sous une autre forme, qu'il ne faut aimer Dieu *contre* personne et que dans l'histoire il ne faut pas aimer les dons de la grâce *contre* les peuples qui sont venus au monde avant Jésus-Christ." [20]

It was interesting and surprising to discover that the psychological validity of Claudel's symbolism had been independently confirmed in the work of Carl Gustav Jung. Péguy's insistence on a heritage accumulated over the centuries and from various cultures also finds support in Jung's writings. In his essays on analytical psychology, Jung compares the structure of the soul of modern man to that of a house, the top floor of which was built in the nineteenth century, the ground level in perhaps the sixteenth, that on a Roman foundation, and so on, until continued excavation uncovers at the bottom remains from the Stone Age. Because of this "soul structure," man has access to what Jung calls the *collective unconscious*, which is, according to him, a very real and vital force. In a chapter entitled "The Structure of the Unconscious" Jung writes:

> All the fundamental instincts and all fundamental forms of thought are collective. Everything that all men agree in regarding as universal is collective as well as all that is universally understood, expressed and done. [21]

Jung goes on to say that it is through identification with the collective psyche that *prophetic inspiration* and a *sense of renewal* of life are attained. If one accepts this thesis, then *ancienne France*, far from being a narrow concept, represents universal instincts and understandings, and in this sense itself partakes of the universal.

George Painter, in *André Gide: A Critical Biography* (New York: Atheneum, 1968), suggests that, in a narrow sense at least, the elder brother in Gide's parable is Claudel. The degree of Claudel's intolerance is humorously illustrated in an anecdote Painter relates. Claudel was having lunch one day when he spied a flaming *crêpe*. "That," he exclaimed with delight, "is how Gide's soul will burn in hell."

[20] *Eve*, "Notes," p. 1527.
[21] Carl Gustav Jung, *Two Essays on Analytical Psychology*, trans. by R. F. C. Hull, Balligen series XX (N.Y.: Pantheon, 1953), p. 274.

Surely Péguy's identification with the collective unconscious was a source of renewal in his writing, and perhaps even of prophetic inspiration.

If I have discussed the nature of *ancienne France* at some length it is because I find this concept more complex than Claudel's *moyen âge*. For Claudel, the Middle Ages served as a sort of circular framework within which were contained certain values and attitudes which he admired. In the case of *ancienne France,* on the contrary, these values are themselves the warp and woof of the fabric; that is, they constitute *ancienne France.*

Specifically, they consist of the simplest of virtues. The first of these is the ethic of work. We have already seen how this ethic was inculcated in Péguy as a child, and expressed in the early *Jeanne d'Arc.* Work in *ancienne France* is a sacrament:

> Ces ouvriers ne servaient pas. Ils travaillaient. Ils avaient un honneur, absolu, comme c'est le propre d'un honneur. Il fallait qu'un bâton de chaise fût bien fait ... Il fallait qu'il fût bien fait lui-même, en lui-même, pour lui-même, dans son être même. Une tradition, venue, montée du plus profond de la race, une histoire, un absolu, un honneur voulait que ce bâton de chaise fût bien fait. Toute partie, dans la chaise, qui ne se voyait pas, était exactement aussi parfaitement faite que ce qu'on voyait. C'est le principe même des cathédrales.[22]

This honor, found in a job well done was for Péguy "le plus beau de tous les honneurs, le plus chrétien."[23]

Earlier I had said that nowhere in Péguy's writing do we find Claudel's fascination for the rite and pageantry of the Middle Ages. Yet in a different way, the doctrine of work in itself constituted rite: "Tout était un rythme et un rite et une cérémonie depuis le petit lever. Tout était un évènement; sacré. Tout était une tradition, un enseignement, tout était la plus sainte habitude."[24] There was, in those days, a sort of contract between man and fate, "... et à ce contract, le sort n'avait jamais manqué avant l'inauguration des

---

[22] "Argent," II, p. 1105.
[23] Ibid.
[24] Ibid., p. 1106.

temps modernes." [25] All of this represented to Péguy "le système même de la réalité," as opposed to "cette méchanique, cet automatique économique du monde moderne." [26]

Moreover, and again in keeping with the integral aspect of Péguy's thought, the honor of work comprehended all other honors: "Tous les honneurs convergaient en cet honneur. Une décence, et une finesse de langage. Un respect du foyer. Un sens de respect, de tous les respects, de l'être même du respect." [27] The good and faithful worker is also by extension the good father, the faithful husband. Péguy writes in *Le Porche* of the humble peasant who is, in actuality, Péguy himself.* The peasant works for his children, of course, "Car on ne travaille jamais que pour les enfants." [28] And he thinks, a little sadly, of the day when he will lie next to his forebears, when his place will be taken by his children. Perhaps he will leave them without land, but they will at least inherit his good tools, which Péguy enumerates lovingly, and with the tools, far more:

> Avec ses outils sûrement et sa race et son sang ses enfants hériteront.
> Ce qui est au-dessus de tout.
> La bénédiction de Dieu qui est sur sa maison et sur sa race.
> La grâce de Dieu qui vaut plus que tout.
> Il le sait bien.
> Qui est sur le pauvre et sur celui qui travaille.
> Et qui élève bien ses enfants. [29]

His place — all of his places — will be filled by his children. In the following passage we see how inextricably these simple functions are linked together:

> Ses deux gars le remplaceront, ses enfants tiendront sa place sur la terre.
> Quand il n'y sera plus.
> Sa place dans la paroisse et sa place dans la forêt.
> Sa place dans l'église et sa place dans la maison.

---

[25] Ibid., p. 1126.
[26] Ibid., p. 1127.
[27] Ibid., p. 1106.
* He even mentions the ages and sex of the peasant's children, which correspond to those of his own.
[28] *Le Porche*, p. 540.
[29] Ibid., p. 543.

> Sa place dans le bourg et sa place dans la vigne.
> Et sur la plaine et sur le coteau et dans la vallée.
> Sa place dans la chrétienté. Enfin. Quoi.
> Sa place d'homme et sa place de chrétien.
> Sa place de paroissien, sa place de laboureur.
> Sa place de paysan.
> Sa place de père.
> Sa place de Lorrain et de Français.
> Car c'est des places, grand Dieu, qu'il faut qui soient tenues.
> Et il faut que tout cela continue. [30]

This is what Péguy means when he speaks of his "inébranlable attachement à la vieille culture, qui en effet était la vieille vertu..." [31]

Linked to the ethic of work is that of poverty, for God bestows his blessing on "the poor and on him who works." Jeanne's poverty, as noted in Chapter I, was not accidental, but a necessary qualification for her task. There is, moreover, a very great distinction between "poverty" and "misery." In *ancienne France* misery had existed, to be sure, but in nothing like the extent that it exists in the modern world. Poverty, on the other hand, was almost universal. "On ne gagnait rien, on vivait de rien, on était heureux." [32] In those days, "Il était entendu que celui qui voulait sortir de la pauvreté risquait de tomber dans la misère." [33] Clearly Péguy is contrasting simple lack of wealth with the spiritual misery that often accompanies the pursuit of wealth.

Modern misery is for him, in fact, directly traceable to the dominance of the bourgeoisie, and with that, to the reign of money: "Tout le mal est venu de la bourgeoisie. Toute l'abérration, tout le crime. C'est la bourgeoisie capitaliste qui a infecté le peuple." [34]

Materialism, an aberration itself, leads to other aberrations. When the savings-bank approach to life is applied to learning, for example, man falls into the sort of scientism Péguy deplored, imagining he can catalogue or "know" all. On the contrary, it is the child who "knows": *

---

[30] Ibid., p. 544.
[31] "Argent," II, p. 1114.
[32] Ibid., p. 1107.
[33] Ibid., p. 1127.
[34] Ibid., p. 1108.

* Péguy here anticipates St. Exupéry and *Le Petit Prince*. Had the pilot

> On envoie les enfants á l'école, dit Dieu.
> Je pense que c'est pour oublier le peu qu'ils savent.
> ...
> On croit que les enfants ne savent rien.
> Et que les parents et que les grandes personnes savent quelque chose.
> Or je vous dis, c'est le contraire.
> (C'est toujours le contraire.)
> Ce sont les parents, ce sont les grandes personnes qui ne savent rien.
> Et ce sont les enfants qui savent
> Tout.[35]

Péguy evokes all these simple virtues of a time gone by with nostalgia. But had he stopped there, he would have done no more than make what he had earlier called *un retracé historique* rather than a *remémoration*. It was not with regret but for renewal that he turned to the past. For *ancienne France* contained forces he felt very *present* — the restorative forces of the saints and heroes.

Théodore Quoniam, in *La Pensée de Péguy* comments on the remarkable vitality of the saint and hero, the quality in both which elicited Péguy's admiration:

> La force impulsive, irrésistible, qui pousse à des actions héroïques devient chez le saint exigence de dépassement. Dépassement équilibré dans les voies de la spiritualité, mais qui rend l'homme toujours plus présent à lui-même et aux exigences de l'appel auquel il répond... Or justement le héros et plus encore le saint portent en eux une exigence de dépassement; leur conscience n'est pas fermée sur une limite; à chaque niveau supérieur qu'ils atteignent, un appel retentit en eux, les portant à pousser plus loin, á s'engager toujours davantage, à assumer le risque. Le propre du christianisme n'est-il point d'avoir trouvé leur destination à la triple grandeur de l'homme, la mort, la misère, le risque?[36]

Here Quoniam stresses what I had earlier pointed out — the need to be *present* and to assume and live with risk.

---

shown his *boa fermé, dessin numéro 1* to Péguy surely the latter would not, like *les grandes personnes*, have mistaken it for a hat.

[35] *Les Saints innocents*, p. 785.
[36] Théodore Quoniam, *La Pensée de Péguy* (Paris: Bordas, 1967), p. 107.

The communion of the saints is an important theme in Claudel, frequently alluded to in *L'Annonce*. It is possibly even more important in Péguy, for the spirit of the saints pervades every aspect of life, present, past, future. The Christian, Péguy writes, sees himself as ever under the protection of all the patrons and saints who have gone before. And he continues:

> Ou plutôt, ou exactement, le chrétien se voit dans le passé, dans le présent, dans le futur. Car il se voit dans une véritable, dans une réelle éternité. Le chrétien se regarde pour ainsi dire ... sous le regard, sous la considération, sous la protection de tous les saints passés, ensemble, et ensemble de tous les saints présents, et ensemble de tous les saints futurs et à venir. C'est même ce que l'on nomme la communion des saints ... La communion des saints procède d'une éternité, de la réelle éternité. Elle peut ensuite se distribuer dans les temps, et notamment dans et entre les passé(s), présent et futur(s). [37]

These spiritual presences were totally real to Péguy. Like Dona Prouhèze, he too had a guardian angel, "plus malin que moi." As he confided to his friend Peslouan, he had twenty times been ready to sin, and twenty times circumstances — which he attributed to his angel's watchfulness — intervened.[38] That the modern world should be oblivious to these presences was just one more of his griefs against it. "Misérables modernes ... Est-il assez évident que ces malheureux ont voulu laïciser la communion?"[39] He wrote to Louis Baillet as early as 1902 that he had abandoned his plans to have *Jeanne d'Arc* produced, explaining, "L'âge où nous vivons est trop barbare pour que cette œuvre ait un public."[40]

Péguy regards the function of the saint very much as does Claudel. The saint does not save himself alone, but brings a crowd of sinners behind him. This idea must have appealed to Péguy on an emotional level, for it constituted a sort of heavenly socialism. As Mallard points out:

---

[37] "Clio," p. 219.
[38] Jean Delaporte, *Péguy dans son Temps et dans le Nôtre* (Paris: Union générale d'éditions, 1944), p. 299.
[39] "Clio," II, p. 223.
[40] *Lettres et Entretiens*, p. 49.

> ...la sainteté est une fonction de salut, le saint gagne à Dieu un crédit par la surabondance de ses mérites et ceux-ci se déversent entre les pécheurs. Les saints paient pour autrui et dans leur éternité bienheureuse, se mêlent ainsi activement à la vie de leurs frères. Il existe donc un socialisme de l'au-delà, d'après lequel chaque saint mène à Dieu une colonne de pécheurs.[41]

The liberation which Jeanne or sainte Genevière achieve for their people is both temporal and eternal. In the conclusion of *Eve* Péguy envisions Jeanne in Paradise with the army of souls she commands: "Heureux ceux d'entre nous qui la verront paraître, / Le regard plus ouvert que d'une âme d'enfant, / Quand ce grand général et ce chef triomphant / Rassemblera sa troupe aux pieds de notre maître."[42]

If the saint is necessary to the sinner, the latter is likewise necessary to the saint. God warns of the danger of concentrating on saint Louis to the exclusion of Joinville. "Si l'on oubliait les pécheurs, il n'en resterait pas beaucoup. / Peu de saints, beaucoup de pécheurs, comme partout. / Mais il faut ce grand cortège de pécheurs. / Pour accompagner ces quelques saints. Il faut penser aussi au sire de Joinville."[43]

Interestingly, although both Claudel and Péguy quite naturally deal more with the saints of France than those of other lands, Péguy would have liked to place them (like their country) in a special category. This is quite evident in the long discussion between Madame Gervaise and Jeannette in *Le Mystère de la Charité*. Jeannette condemns one of the first saints, Peter, for his denial of Christ, and insists over and again that the French saints, whom she names at length, would never have denied him, nor, for that matter, would the simple French peasants: "Jamais les hommes de ce pays-ci, jamais des saints de ce pays-ci, jamais des simples chrétiens même de nos pays ne l'auraient abandonné. Jamais des chevaliers français, jamais des paysans français..."[44] Through Madame Gervaise Péguy quite properly rebukes Jeannette's chauvinism, but his heart, in secret, appears to be with her.

---

[41] Mallard, p. 118.
[42] *Eve*, p. 1173.
[43] *Les Saints innocents*, p. 720.
[44] *Le Mystère de la Charité*, p. 499.

The saints for Péguy can be divided into two categories: "Il y a ceux qui sortent des justes. Et il y a ceux qui sortent des pécheurs," [45] and "Les saints de Dieu sortent de deux écoles. / De l'école du juste et de l'école du pécheur. / De la vacillante école du péché. / Heureusement que c'est toujours Dieu qui est le maître d'école." [46] He does not give specific examples, but one might assume that sainte Geneviève, "la sainte la plus grande après sainte Marie," [47] would belong with the saints of the just. Certainly Jeanne belongs in the second category, for as we have seen, she is consumed by doubts, distress, rebellion, and Péguy described the two kinds of saints as: "ceux qui n'ont jamais inspiré d'inquiétudes sérieuses / Et ceux qui ont inspiré une inquiétude mortelle." [48]

The two kinds of saints join to plot against God:

> Car tous ensemble ils passent tout leur temps toute leur
>   sainte journée à comploter contre Dieu.
> Devant Dieu.
> Pour que pied à pied la Justice
> Pas à pas cède à la Miséricorde.
>
> Ils font violence à Dieu. Comme des bons soldats ils
>   luttent pied à pied,
> (Ils font la guerre à la justice.
> Ils sont bien forcés)
> Pour le salut des âmes périclitantes. [49]

In their battle they have the protection of two patrons, who are none other than the Virgin herself and Jesus Christ, her son. With this sort of backing the saints, of course, win their very necessary victory, "Car s'il n'y avait que la Justice et si la Miséricorde ne s'en mêlait pas, / qui serait sauvé?" [50]

Needless to say, this is God's little joke (Péguy's God always keep his sense of humor) which he tells on himself, for he is really on the side of the saints. As he says, "Comment serais-je moins tendre que saint Louis. Comme lui je tremble / Pour leur salut." [51]

---

[45] *Le Porche*, p. 618.
[46] Ibid., p. 619.
[47] *La Tapisserie de sainte Geneviève*, p. 876.
[48] *Le Porche*, p. 618.
[49] Ibid., p. 619.
[50] Ibid., p. 612.
[51] *Les Saints innocents*, p. 734.

And he compares the intolerance (for Péguy's God is also tolerant) of the Pharisees with the compassion of the saint for the sinner:

> Les Pharisiens veulent toujours de la perfection
> Pour les autres. Chez les autres.
> Mais le saint qui veut de la perfection pour lui-même
> En lui-même
> Et qui cherche et qui peine dans le labeur et dans les larmes
> Et qui obtient quelquefois quelque perfection,
> Le saint est moins difficile pour les autres.
> Il est moins exigeant pour les autres. Il sait ce que c'est. [52]

The familiarity with which Péguy treats the saints, almost as if they were personal friends, is in striking contrast to Claudel's treatment. As we saw in Chapter IV, Claudel is interested, not in the historical person, but in the "essence" of the saint. His sainte Geneviève, for example, represents the indomitable spirit of the French people face to face with a mortal enemy. In Péguy, on the other hand, the saint is first of all a human being, attached to a certain time and place — his Present.

Earlier I had discussed Jung's theory of the collective unconscious, and his contention that it is through identification with this collective heritage that a sense of renewal is attained. Péguy certainly makes that identification — with his attachment to *ancienne France,* his feelings about the communion of the saints. But always, having made the identification, he then particularizes, and gives to his inner experience individual, human form. Quoniam observed: "Chez Péguy le collectif s'individualise toujours, s'incarne et permet ainsi le dialogue direct, vivant." [53] Thus we come to know Jeanne or saint Louis just as we might "know" a character in a novel, each saint emerging as a distinct individual.

For all their saintliness, Péguy's saints, like the poet himself, are very much this-world oriented. In Claudel one always feels that the vision of his characters, saints or not, is focused on the life to come: they are *in* but not quite *of* this world. Rodrigue, for example, accepts his final captivity almost with indifference; he is already free, and living on a higher plane. Anne Vercors is so other-world directed that he finds in the death of his wife and daughter

---

[52] Ibid., p. 735.
[53] Quoniam, p. 24.

a source of calm joy. Péguy's saints, by contrast, are sorely troubled by the misery they see and exert all their efforts to combat it. One might say that where Claudel's characters are struggling to reach the Eternal, Péguy's saints are striving to inject a little heaven into this poor earth.

The emphasis on the flesh and blood person who is the saint is strikingly illustrated in a very long section of *Le Mystère de la Charité* in which Péguy describes the mother of God as she follows her son to his crucifixion. The terms in which Péguy describes her have offended some of his critics, for this is not the tender, ageless woman as she is usually represented in religious art (Michelangelo's *Pietà,* for example).

> Elle pleurait, elle pleurait, elle était devenue laide.
> En trois jours.
> Elle était devenue affreuse.
> Affreuse à voir.
> Si laide, si affreuse.
> Qu'on se serait moqué d'elle.
> Sûrement.
> Si elle n'avait pas été la mère du condamné.
>
> Elle pleurait, elle pleurait. Ses yeux, ses pauvres yeux.
> Ses pauvres yeux étaient rougis de larmes.
> Et jamais ils ne verraient bien clair.
> Après.[54]

There is absolutely no disrespect in Péguy's treatment of the Virgin. Quite the contrary. This is just one more example of his insistence on the union of carnal and spiritual. As Péguy explains, all creatures lack something: the angels, who are pure, are not carnal; Man, who is carnal, is not pure. But the Virgin is the exception: "... et à elle au contraire il ne manque rien ... Car étant charnelle elle est pure. Mais, étant pure, aussi elle est charnelle."[55] Claudel's disembodied essences would not have pleased Péguy any more than Péguy's accent on physical realities would have pleased Claudel.

---

[54] *Le Mystère de la Charité,* p. 463.
[55] *Le Porche,* p. 576.

This brings us to another area of comparison between Claudel and Péguy: the theme of suffering in the works of each. In Claudel the various characters talk a great deal about suffering, but *physically* they suffer very little. The Jesuit priest, crucified on the mast, gives thanks for his own suffering and prays that Rodrigue, his brother, may also suffer. But he says not a word about his pain. The nail-pierced hands of the Princess do not prevent her from ministering to the dying Tête d'Or. And notice how poetically Violaine reveals her illness to Jacques: "Connais le feu dont je suis dévorée," and he, in turn, refers to the leprous spot as "cette fleur d'argent dont votre chair est blasonnée."[56] Violaine's leprosy, in fact, is less a physical disease than the symbol of the suffering she had undertaken in expiation for the sin that surrounds her, as she herself explains to Mara.

How different is the discussion of leprosy in *Le Mystère des Saints innocents!* Joinville tells saint Louis he would rather have committed thirty mortal sins than contract the disease. And God considers this response with charity. After all, he says, it is not Joinville who loves God thirty times less, but the extraordinary saint Louis who loves him thirty times more. Moreover, the disease of which they speak is not some theoretic possibility, but a reality which they both knew. As God says, "Cette lèpre dont ils parlaient et d'être lépreux / Ce n'était pas une lèpre d'invention et une lèpre d'exercice / ... Mais c'était la réelle lèpre et ils parlaient de l'avoir, eux-mêmes, réellement."[57] And then God, in a long passage, describes the awful ravages of the disease. A short quotation will suffice to show the gruesome precision of the description:

Cette sèche moisissure blanche qui gagne de proche en proche
Et qui mord comme avec des dents de souris,
Et qui fait d'un homme le rebut et la fuite de l'homme,
Et qui détruit un corps comme une granuleuse moisissure
Et qui pousse sur le corps ces affreuses blanches lèvres,
Ces affreuses lèvres sèches de plaies.[58]

It is clear that for Péguy, at least, there is nothing whatsoever "poetic" about suffering.

---

[56] *L'Annonce*, p. 174.
[57] *Les Saints innocents*, p. 724.
[58] Ibid.

Both Claudel and Péguy would agree that happiness, in the ordinary usage of the word, is incompatible with salvation. Péguy observes in his essay on Hugo, "... il n'a jamais été donné à un homme de faire à la fois son bonheur et son salut." [59] Nor does he deny that suffering may be redemptive. He states as much in the opening lines of *La Tapisserie de sainte Geneviève*: "Comme Dieu ne sait rien que par pauvre misère, / Il fallut qu'elle vît sa ville endolorie," [60] and he enumerates the things which the saint must endure seeing, and having seen, suffer. Even so, Péguy's concept of suffering is different and more complex than that of Claudel. As Jeanne tells Madame Gervaise, "Il y a une souffrance utile, et une souffrance inutile. Il y a une souffrance féconde, et une souffrance inféconde." [61]

Jean Delaporte, in his book, *Péguy dans son Temps et dans le nôtre,* comments on the nature and causes of Jeanne's suffering: "La lamentation de Jeanne rappelle les gémissements de Job et de Jérémie; le temps présent est mauvais, et derrière cette face actuelle se déchiffre la puissance du 'Mal universel'." [62] Herein lies the difference between Claudel and Péguy's concepts of suffering. Many of Claudel's characters *choose* to suffer — this is certainly the case with the early Violaine, Dona Prouhèze, Orian — they taste a sweetness of renunciation in their voluntary sacrifices. Such an attitude would have seemed, I believe, both presumptuous and dangerously ascetic to Péguy. For Jeanne resists, rebels, before she finally accepts the suffering she cannot avoid. She does not want any part of the horror of war, she longs to be back on her father's farm, performing the simple tasks she had loved. She suffers because she is constrained to suffer, seeing, as Delaporte suggests, in the evils of her world a manifestation of Evil itself. In my own opinion, this concept of suffering is more authentically Christian than that developed by Claudel, and which, in a sense, he *needed* to develop to explain particular events in his own life. To accept suffering with grace and patience when it is inevitable is certainly part of the Christian ethic, but to seek it out actively may be self-destructive, and self-destruction is expressly forbidden.

---

[59] "Note conjointe sur Victor Hugo," II, p. 1350.
[60] *La Tapisserie de sainte Geneviève*, p. 846.
[61] *Le Mystère de la Charité*, p. 431.
[62] Delaporte, p. 242.

I should like to consider now the other spiritual force on which Péguy drew in his effort to re-vitalize his world, and that, of course, is the hero. He (or, perhaps in Péguy's case the feminine pronoun would be more appropriate) was intimately linked to the saint. Both are forces of re-creation, both respond to a profound need of the poet himself. Mallard observes:

> Dès ses premières années et un peu plus tard dans "Notre Jeunesse" il éprouve un besoin d'héroïsme... peut-être (sans doute) un besoin de sainteté. Il a la nostalgie de pureté absolue des premières âges du monde, de la "création continue"... car pour Péguy, la vie est une perpétuelle création.[63]

and of Péguy himself Mallard says: "[il] nous propose un modèle dans lequel héroïsme et sainteté confondent harmonieusement leur marche."[64]

Quoniam, in a chapter entitled "Recensement des Valeurs," discusses the values which the hero symbolized for Péguy:

> Le héros est une incarnation de la Valeur Noblesse, car il est, par destination, au service de la Justice. C'est avant tout l'homme né pour le combat loyal. Il ne doit donc pécher ni par faiblesse de cœur ni par dureté de cœur, mesure difficile à tenir. Il semble modelé à l'image de ce paysage doux en ce sens de fermeté qui est la véritable douceur.[65]

The hero embodies a certain health, youth, gaiety and joy (which has nothing to do with "happiness") which can perhaps best be summed up by a word often used to describe a quality of the Cornelian hero — *allégresse*.* Quoniam had used the word *douceur* in connection with the hero, and he is correct. Lifted above the crowd, the hero yet retains about him a simplicity, tenderness and innocence that stand in direct opposition to that other concept of

---

[63] Mallard, p. 21.
[64] Ibid., p. 116.
[65] Quoniam, p. 107.

* Péguy admired these very qualities in Corneille's theater: "Corneille s'était donné ce monde, ce peuple de l'espérance, cette invention de nouveau, cette innovation de la nouveauté. Il s'était donné cette enfance et cette jeunesse." "Note Conjointe sur M. Descartes," p. 1412.

the hero, the Nietzschean *Übermensch*. Gillet, in his published lectures, Claudel-Péguy, observes, "Péguy, c'est l'anti-Nietzsche, l'antidote parfait, le contraire du surhomme." [66]

This concept of the hero is in the tradition of the old *chanson de geste*. In his essay on Descartes, Péguy discusses at length the system which the hero represents, and by which he lives. In this system it is not who wins but how the battle is fought that counts: *

> Dans ce système de pensée la bataille passe avant la victoire et la mort même n'est rien au prix de la correction du combat... Ce n'est pas seulement le système de la loyauté. C'est le système de l'héroïsme. Et c'est le système de l'honneur. Il est tout ramassé dans le code du duel... C'est le système de penseé de la chevalerie, et notamment de la chevalerie française. [67]

It is only one step from the hero to the Just War, for that concept grew of the code of the duel. According to Péguy there are two kinds of wars — one between honorable opponents, and basically a struggle *for* honor (at the level of the duel, he cites the example of Rodrigue and Don Gomès and on an even higher spiritual plane, that of Polyeucte and Sévère). It is certainly in keeping with his thinking that the French — *people inventeur des Croisades* — should excel in the Just War. The two types of war are clearly distinguishable (although historically, Péguy admits, neither kinds has existed in its pure form): "... l'une est la lutte pour l'honneur, et l'autre la lutte pour le pouvoir... Il y a une race de la guerre qui étant pour l'honneur est tout même pour l'éternel. Et il y a une race de la guerre qui étant pour la domination est uniquement pour le temporel." [68] In Homer, for example, the Trojan war begins as a war of honor, a series of personal duels which should determine the final outcome. But then Ulysses changes the character of the conflict

---

[66] Gillet, p. 211.

* It should be noted that in his own life Péguy followed the example of his heroes and heroines. His desire to walk uncompromised, *les mains pures*, and his resulting intransigence on moral issues were responsible for many of his personal and political difficulties.

[67] "Note conjointe sur M. Descartes," II, p. 1420.

[68] Ibid., p. 1421.

— "il fausse tout le système" [69] — by his use of trickery, the Trojan horse. He replaces by this act the system of battle with the system of victory.

Péguy calls the first kind of war, based on the code of the duel, either the Greek or the French "race" of war, the second, the Roman system. The opposition is far-reaching, and again goes back to Christianity:

> Tout est proposition dans le système de la chevalerie. Tout est domination dans le système romain. Tout est requête dans le système chevaleresque. Et tout est conquête dans le système romain.
>
> Dans le système chevaleresque il s'agit de mesurer des valeurs. Dans le système de l'empire il s'agit d'obtenir et de fixer les résultats.

And then, in the same paragraph he writes, with remarkable prescience:

> Pour nous modernes, chez nous l'un est celtique et l'autre est romain. L'un est féodal et l'autre est d'empire. L'un est chrétien et l'autre est romain. Les Français ont excellé dans l'un et les Allemands ont quelquefois excellé dans l'autre et les Japonais paraissent avoir excellé dans l'un et réussi dans l'autre. [70]

This attitude toward a just war explains what might otherwise seem paradoxical — how a Christian can justify war at all. It also illuminates the beautiful passage in *Eve*, which begins with the well-known lines, "Heureux ceux qui sont morts pour la terre charnelle /Mais pourvu que ce fût dans une juste guerre," [71] and which served as his epitaph after his death in what he truly believed to be a just war.

With the exception of Polyeucte (in prose) and saint Louis (in prose and poetry) all the saints and heroes whom Péguy treats at length are women. And this brings up the very important question of the role of woman in his work. As earlier noted, that role is

---

[69] Ibid., p. 1422.
[70] Ibid., p. 1423.
[71] *Eve*, p. 1028.

every bit as important in Péguy as in Claudel, but very different. I had speculated, dangerously, no doubt (for it is always dangerous to try to search out the psychological bases of an author's secret motivations), as to the probable causes for Claudel's attitude toward woman. Péguy's concept of woman also seems linked to his personality and life experience.

Various of Péguy's biographers have dealt with the question, and Robert Vigneault has devoted an entire book — *l'Univers féminin dans l'œuvre de Charles Péguy* — to it. Taking more or less of a Freudian approach, Vigneault comes up with many interesting ideas, although some of his conclusions seem precariously founded. I do not see, for example, the sensuality and sexuality which he finds in the beginning portions of *Le Porche*. Nor do I agree that *Le Porche* ends in an abdication to "*la Mère-Nuit*" who represents, according to Vigneault, the poet's own mother.[72] Writes Vigneault, "*Le Porche* inaugure une puissante affirmation virile, mais finit par une abdication infantile ... où, comme le rappelle ce verset de la dernière page du livre, 'La Mère était là.' "[73] He also attributes Péguy's conversion to socialism to his mother's (negative) influence: "Son expérience socialiste est une noble transposition de sa révolte contre les 'manques d'une enfance étouffante, la valorisation idéologique de ses 'manques individuels.' "[74] It is probably true Péguy's socialism was in part an unconscious rebellion against his mother and her values, but as I tried earlier to show, it was also a positive reaction to the injustices he saw around him.

Even so, there is no denying the tremendous influence both his mother and wife had on him, separately and together — in their continual feuding. Despite the enormous respect Péguy had for the former, as we have seen her through her own words or in descriptions of her by others, she was a formidable figure, frightening when crossed, a woman who "... savait aimer, certes; comme elle savait aussi détester; haïr."[75]

Rousseau, in his *Confessions,* says that he wrote *La Nouvelle Heloïse* with the express intent "... de donner ainsi l'essor en

---

[72] Robert Vigneault, "Espérance et feminité," *L'Univers féminin dans l'œuvre de Charles Péguy* (Montréal: Les Editions Bellarmin, 1967).
[73] Ibid., p. 193.
[74] Vigneault, p. 225.
[75] Isaac, p. 157.

quelque sorte au désir d'aimer que je n'avais pu satisfaire et dont je me sentis dévoré."[76] It is entirely possible that the women in Péguy's work represent his need to give form to the idealized woman he had imagined, but never known. In any case, his saints and heroines display the courage, integrity and purity he had admired in his mother and grandmother, but are also endowed with the gentleness and compassion they — and his wife — had lacked. In Péguy, the woman is mother, comforter, and with Jeanne, adolescent youth. She is never, however, the object of sexual love. Part of the reason for this may stem, very simply, from Péguy's personality, and the childlike purity which the man had retained. M. Saint Clair observes, "Cet enfant austère, qui ne connait pas la tentation, devait préserver chez l'homme une pureté farouche et simple, qui est un des accents les plus émouvants de son génie."[77] Halévy reported that all of Péguy's friends, himself included, had the impression that Péguy was a person almost untouched by sexuality.

Yet Péguy, like Claudel, did have one great love. Her name was Blanche Raphaël, she was Jewish, the daughter of a professor, and she died in 1960. It is of small importance that, in the opinion of Péguy's friends who knew her, she was probably unworthy of his intense devotion, or that, as Delaporte suggests, she welcomed an offer of marriage which "freed" her of Péguy. What is important is that Péguy, the man, remained scrupulously faithful to those principles the poet had enshrined in his verse. He helped arrange her marriage and, although he continued to see her up to the time of his departure for the front, managed to preserve the purity of their relationship. (Vigneault, in fact, attributes the virility he finds in the first part of *Le Porche* to the fact that Blanche was pregnant at the time, and adds that Péguy later preferred her child to his own. Again, this seems to me intriguing but too conjectural. It is difficult to imagine Péguy, like Claudel's heroes [or his heroine, Violaine], having a "soul-child.")

Those few persons who knew of the situation were appalled by the intensity of Péguy's suffering. Unlike Claudel, however, he

---

[76] Jean-Jacques Rousseau, *Œuvres complètes,* Bibliothèque de la Pléiade (Paris: Gallimard, 1962), Confessions, Livre IX, p. 431.
[77] M. St. Clair, "Charles Péguy," *Galerie Privée* (Paris: Gallimard, 1947), p. 172.

made no direct reference to this love in his work. Only in the *Quatrains,* which were unpublished during his lifetime (and probably not intended for publication) do we glimpse his agony. The two stanzas which follow are typical:

> Cœur plein d'un seul amour
>   Dissuadé
> O cœur de jour en jour
>   Plus obsédé.
>
> Cœur plein d'un seul amour
>   Désaccordé,
> O cœur de jour en jour
>   Plus hasardé.[78]

If, in Claudel "le péché aussi sert," in Péguy purity, and only purity, is admissible. Gillet is correct when he observes, "Sa poésie a les mains pures. Elle n'est au fond qu'une prière."[79]

Jeanne is the pure hero-saint of youth. Sainte Geneviève is her counterpart in great age. But Eve is the embodiment of all human suffering through the ages. She suffers because she knows that she, through her weakness, is responsible for the anguish of the human condition. And she suffers more than any other because she alone has known the perfection of Eden, "la jeunesse du monde," beautifully evoked in the first part of the poem. Gillet refers to her as "une sorte de femme éternelle, d'Ewiges Weibliche, une espèce de vieille Parque perdue dans ses souvenirs et qui file indéfiniment... les destins innombrables de ses filles et de ses fils."[80]

Jesus salutes her suffering with compassion:

> Et moi je vous salue, ô première femme
> Et la plus malheureuse et la plus décevante
> Et la plus immobile et la plus émouvante
> Aïeule aux longs cheveux, mère de Notre Dame.[81]

It is, indeed, out of pity for Eve and all her children that Jesus came to this earth, and becoming man, took on all the sorrows of the human race:

---

[78] *Les Quatrains,* p. 1284.
[79] Gillet, p. 221.
[80] Ibid., p. 214.
[81] *Eve,* p. 947.

> Vous n'avez enfanté qu'une race plaintive,
> Tantôt rivée au sol, tantôt victorieuse.
> Tantôt martyre et sainte, et sage ou curieuse,
> O mère et c'est ma race et la race captive.[82]

If Eve had once known absolute purity, Mary, mother of God, was the only human being (excepting, of course, her son) to remain pure, and it is to her that Péguy turns for help in his darkest hours — when his children are near death, when his heart is torn and he doubts his ability to continue. In *Le Porche de la deuxième Vertu* we saw her as a woman and mother. In *Les Tapisseries de Notre Dame* she is the Virgin, ascended into heaven in all her glory. For this reader at least, nothing Péguy wrote rivals the rather short "Présentation de la Beauce à Notre Dame de Chartres" for sheer poetic beauty and depth of feeling. The poem, which forms part of *Les Tapisseries*, recounts Péguy's pilgrimage to the cathedral of Chartres to offer thanks to Our Lady for the recovery of his son. The pilgrim presents himself to the Virgin:

> Etoile du matin, inaccessible reine,
> Voici que nous marchons vers votre illustre tour,
> Et voici le plateau de notre pauvre amour,
> Et voici l'océan de notre immense peine.[83]

The lone steeple of Chartres rising over the Beauce seems to Péguy like a beautiful ear of grain, symbol of fecundity,* of the renewal that the Virgin, as the mother of Christ, represents. The cathedral, filled with the invisible presence of Mary, becomes a sort of spiritual center to which the poet's soul is drawn, and where it finds at length peace:

> Voici l'axe et la ligne et la géante fleur.
> Voici la dure pente et le contentement.
> Voici l'exactitude et le consentement.
> Et la sévère larme, ô reine de douleur.[84]

---

[82] Ibid., p. 953.
[83] *Tapisserie de Notre Dame*, p. 896.
* One is reminded by this image, which Péguy repeats several times — "C'est la gerbe et le blé qui ne périra point," etc. — of a similar metaphor that occurs in the last act of *L'Annonce*, when Pierre says he will crown his church with a statue of Violaine, "... les mains croisées sur la poitrine, comme l'épi à demi-prisonnier de ses téguments." *L'Annonce*, II, p. 209.
[84] Ibid., p. 903.

Péguy's love for and gratitude toward the Virgin stem from the fact that it was she who, as he had confided to Lotte, saved him from the dealiest sin, despair. Speaking of the peasant who confides his children to the Virgin's care, Péguy encourages all of us to do the same. In the beautiful description of the mother of God which follows — and I quote only a fragment — we see how she incorporates all the virtues and values the poet was trying to "re-present."

> Alors il faut prendre son courage à deux mains.
> Et s'adresser directement à celle qui est au-dessus de tout.
>
> A celle qui est infiniment grande.
> Parce qu'elle est infiniment petite.
> Infiniment humble.
> Une jeune mère.
>
> A celle qui est infiniment jeune.
> Parce qu'elle est infiniment mère.
>
> A celle qui est infiniment joyeuse.
> Parce qu'aussi elle est infiniment douleureuse.
>
> A celle qui est toute Grandeur et toute Foi.
> Parce qu'aussi elle est toute Charité.
>
> A celle qui est toute Foi et toute Charité.
> Parce qu'aussi elle est toute **Espérance**. [85]

It is significant that while the words *Foi* and *Charité* appear in ordinary type, Espérance is set off in boldface.

This brings me to the last and dominant theme I should like to discuss in connection with Péguy's re-presentation of *ancienne France*. In the conclusion of Chapter III I had said that with *Le Porche* Péguy rediscovered the possibility of hope. But, like Moses, although he might lead others to the Promised Land, he could not himself enter. For it was precisely during the time that he was writing *Le Porche* and *Le Mystère des Saints innocents* that his own distress was most acute. It was not until 1912 that he was able to write to Lotte, "Je suis les conseils que Dieu donne dans mes *Inno-*

---

[85] *Le Porche*, p. 569.

cents. Ce que j'y exprimais, je ne l'avais jamais pratiqué. Maintenant je m'abandonne." [86]

Hope becomes possible through the intervention of Christ. In a lovely and extended metaphor Péguy envisions four flotillas setting out on the ocean of God's just wrath. The flag ship is Christ, his folded hands, the prow. The first flotilla is the *Pater Noster*, the prayer which Jesus taught us and which constitutes, says God, "une barrière que ma colère et peut-être ma justice ne franchira jamais." [87] The second flotilla is the *Ave Maria*; the third, all other prayers, spoken, silent, formal, personal. But the fourth flotilla (and here again we find Péguy's insistence that no one be lost) is composed of all the unsaid prayers — the secret movements in men's hearts of which even they may be unaware.

Even with this fleet at his disposal, man often finds it difficult to hope. For as God says, "On peut lui demander beaucoup de cœur, beaucoup de charité, beaucoup de sacrifice / ... Mais ce qu'on ne peut pas lui demander, sacredié, c'est un peu d'espérance." [88] And then he continues, developing a related idea:

Un peu de confiance, quoi, un peu de détente,
Un peu de remise, un peu d'abandonnement dans mes mains,
Un peu de désistement. Il se raidit tout le temps.
Or toi, ma fille la nuit, tu réussis, quelquefois, tu obtiens
   quelquefois cela.
De l'homme rebelle. [89]

Now, as we have seen before, there is a continual insistence on simplicity in Péguy (for it is Satan, not God, who complicates). Here there is an interesting comparison with Claudel. It is through a monumental effort — consider *Art Poétique* and the *Odes* — that the poet attains, even momentarily, the Eternal, and earns the right, so to speak, to hope. It is through the act of abandoning himself entirely in God's hand that Péguy finds hope. And he explains the basis for this hope through the simplest of parables. When you were a child, he says, and your mother sent you to the store to buy certain items, you didn't begin by telling the grocer all sorts of

---

[86] *Lettres et Entretiens*, p. 51.
[87] *Le Mystère de la Charité*, p. 696.
[88] Ibid., p. 684.
[89] Ibid.

fantasies; you repeated to him just what your mother told you to say. In the same way, Péguy says, "Jésus Christ, mon enfant, n'est pas venu pour nous conter des fariboles." [90] God gave his son a very definite commission, and Jesus relayed the message to us exactly as it had been given to him.

> Il ne s'est pas mis à nous raconter des choses extraordinaires.
> Rien n'est aussi simple que la parole de Dieu.
> Il ne nous a dit que des choses fort ordinaires.
> Très ordinaires.
> L'incarnation, le salut, la rédemption, la parole de Dieu.
> Trois ou quatre mystères.
> La prière, les sept sacrements.
> Rien n'est aussi simple que la grandeur de Dieu. [91]

Instead of torturing and rebuking himself in the long night hours, and sleepless, making fruitless examinations of conscience, man has but to accept the word of God confidently: "Il faut croire en lui, qui est d'espèrer. / Il faut avoir confiance en Dieu, il a bien eu confiance en nous." [92] Péguy's entire religious outlook is summarized in the few lines that follow:

Or, mon enfant, s'il en est ainsi, si c'est ainsi que nous
    devons entendre Jésus.
Que nous devons entendre Dieu.
Littéralement.
Au pied de la lettre.
Rigoureusement, simplement, pleinement, exactement, sainement.
Au ras du mur.
Alors mon enfant quel tremblement, quel commandement d'espéran-
    [ce.
Quelle ouverture, quel saisissement despérance. Quel écrase-
    ment. Les paroles sont là. [93]

    We must, in effect, follow literally the teachings of Christ, and become as the little children. Once more the difference between Claudel and Péguy is remarkable. Claudel, in awe and wonder at the beauty of God's universe, would capture it all "dans les im-

---

[90] *Le Porche*, p. 598.
[91] Ibid., p. 599.
[92] Ibid., p. 603.
[93] Ibid., p. 605.

menses rets de ma connaissance." God, speaking in *Les Saints innocents,* enumerates in a way that would have appealed to Claudel all the beauties of his world — the forests, seas, stars, the cathedrals rising to his glory, the martyr's sacrifice. But then he comes back to the most beautiful thing that he, God, knows, which is also the simplest: "Je n'a'i jamais vu rien de si drôle et par conséquent je ne connais rien de si beau dans le monde / que cet enfant qui s'endort en faisant sa prière / (Que ce petit être qui s'endort de confiance) / Et qui mélange son *Notre Père* avec son *Je vous salue Marie.* [94] We, too, must follow the child's example, for as Jesus counsels in *Eve,* "Celui-là seul qui met son front sur mes genoux / Est seul maître du temps et seul maître du lieu." [95]

Hope is the figure of the Christ child, tenderly evoked in *Eve,* but by extension, hope is *the child.* For the child represents the spirit of newness, the innocence that we, adults, have lost. There is in childish speech some indefinable charm that an adult cannot even retain long enough to repeat. Listen to a child speak, writes Péguy, "Vous écoutez passer votre ancienne âme." [96]

Hope is the little girl who walks in the long procession of life with her grown sisters, Faith and Charity. But while they walk steadfastly onward, she runs ahead, skips back, goes the distance twenty times over, and never once thinks to husband her energy for the next day: "Ce sont les grandes personnes qui ménagent... La seule enfant Espérance / Est la seule qui ne ménage jamais rien." [97] For little Hope understands that it is the journey and not the destination that counts. "...ce qui importe, / Ce n'est pas d'aller ici ou là, ce n'est pas d'aller quelque part / D'arriver quelque part / Terrestre. C'est d'aller, d'aller, toujours, et (au contraire) de ne pas arriver." [98]

Without Hope, indeed, the weary earthly traveler could wish for no more than eternal repose, "Et de se coucher pour dormir. / Dormir, dormir enfin." [99] Without Hope, God admits, "...ils n'au-

---

[94] *Les Saints innocents,* p. 791.
[95] *Eve,* p. 995.
[96] *Les Saints innocents,* p. 794.
[97] *Le Porche,* p. 647.
[98] Ibid.
[99] *Les Saints innocents,* p. 744.

ront aucun goût pour mon paradis / Et pour la vie éternelle." [100] Paradise itself would be no more than oblivion, "Une grande nuit de clarté / Une grande nuit éternelle." [101]

> Car elle seule, comme elle seule dans les jours de cette terre
> D'une vieille veille fait jaillir un lendemain nouveau.
> Ainsi elle seule des résidus du Jugement et des ruines et du débris du temps
> Fera jaillir une éternité neuve. [102]

Faith, says God, changing metaphors, is the lamp which burns eternally in his sanctuary, and Charity is the good fire one lights in the hearth that the poor may warm themselves. "Mais mon espérance est la fleur et le fruit et la feuille et la branche / Et le rameau et le bourgeon de la fleur / De l'éternité même." [103]

From the passages I have quoted in this chapter it is apparent that Péguy's insistence on simplicity, innocence, newness had an important effect on his verse form, which stands in such contrast to that of Claudel. He speaks in the humble language of the peasant or child, he is often ungrammatical, and like them, who have time at their disposal, he talks at length, developing his thoughts slowly and without much concern for sequential logic. Just as a child may examine a pretty stone, turning it in the sun to catch a ray of light in the vein of quartz, tracing with his finger that other red or green vein, chipping it, perhaps, to discover what is inside, so Péguy, with patient wonder and curiosity, examines every aspect of the beauty he has discovered. His symbols, too, are of the simplest sort — the child, the bud, the ear of grain, the oak tree. Grace is the water, continually renewed and clarified, with which the French gardeners irrigate God's earthly garden, or it is the sap rising in the tree, nourishing each small branch.

There is an extraordinary illustration of this insistence on simplicity — of style, symbol, thought — in the last part of *Les Saints innocents*. Péguy retells the story of Herod's slaughter of the Holy Innocents. And he contemplates in awe the wonderful injustice of

---

[100] Ibid.
[101] Ibid., p. 745.
[102] Ibid., p. 746.
[103] Ibid.

God. These babies, who had never known the name of Jesus, these "enfants laiteux" who were conscious only of the warmth of their mothers' breasts, to them is granted a purity such as not even the most long-suffering saint, through martyrdom, can attain.

> Voici que ces cent quarante-quatre mille innocents.
> Voici que ces cent quarante-quatre mille enfants
> N'ont eu qu'à naître, et rien de plus. Tels sont les
>   mystères, tels sont les secrets.
> Tels sont les jeux, telles sont les inégalités de ma grâce.
> Et le secret apparemment, la secrète accointance
> De ma grâce avec la tendresse et le lait.[104]

The other saints, says God, are the ordinary fruit of their season, and even his son was "harvested" in his thirty-third season. But the Innocents are the first fruits of the season offered in sacrifice to God. They precede the fruit even: "Mais eux simples innocents, / Ils sont avant les fruits mêmes, ils sont la promesse du fruit / ... Ils sont l'honneur d'avril et la douce espérance. / Ils sont l'honneur et des bois et des mois / Ils sont la jeune enfance." [105]

A final comparison between Claudel and Péguy. At the conclusion of *Art Poétique* Claudel shares with the reader his vision of eternal life: "... notre occupation pour l'éternité sera l'accomplissement de notre part dans la perpétration de l'Office, le maintien de notre équilibre toujours nouveau dans un immense tact amoureux de tous nos frères, l'élévation de notre voix dans l'inénarrable gémissement de l'amour." [106] How different from this magnificent, comprehensive vision is the heaven God describes in the concluding stanza, quoted here in its entirety, of *Le Mystère des Saints innocents*:

Tel est mon paradis, dit Dieu. Mon paradis est tout ce
    qu'il y a de plus simple.
Rien n'est aussi dépouillé que mon paradis.
Aram sub ipsam au pied de l'autel même.
Ces simples enfants *jouent* avec leur palme et avec leurs
    couronnes de martyrs.

---

[104] Ibid., p. 809.
[105] Ibid., p. 822.
[106] Claudel, *Art poétique*, p. 204.

Voilà ce qui se passe dans mon paradis. A quoi peut-on
    bien jouer
Avec une palme et des couronnes de martyrs.
Je pense qu'ils jouent au cerceau, dit Dieu, et peut-être
    aux grâces
(du moins, je le pense, car ne croyez point
qu'on me demande jamais la permission)
Et la palme toujours verte leur sert apparemment de bâtonnet. [107]

Le monde moderne, suffering from a sort of spiritual arteriosclerosis, operating on a savings-bank approach to life, dominated by money, opposing its infidelities to fidelity, its dishonors to honor, degrading every *mystique* into *politique,* had almost forgotten that the values and revitalizing forces which Péguy evoked still, indeed, existed. For Péguy, these elements were contained in a concept he called *ancienne France,* and it was this concept in its entirety that he wished to make present once more. *Ancienne France* was for him the best, the most gallant experiment in living Christianity this world has ever seen. The sacrament of work and the integrity of the craftsman, the fidelity of the *foyer,* the self-respect of the poor, the vitality of the hero coupled with the gentle confidence and suffering of the saint, the compassion and purity of woman — all of these elements are assimillable, for Péguy, in the very simple teachings of Christ. If Péguy berates the modern world so harshly, it is only to recall it to what he believed to be the very source of life, hope through Christ.

In a day when Despair sneers at a troubled world, Péguy offers an alternative. His work stands as a monument to Hope; a renaissance, a veritable re-creation. It is in their separate achievements of this common goal — the poetic formulation of a doctrine of hope — that Claudel and Péguy finally meet.

---

[107] *Les Saints innocents,* p. 823.

BIBLIOGRAPHY

BOOKS BY PAUL CLAUDEL

Œuvres complètes, 28 vols. Paris: Gallimard, 1950-1967.
Œuvre poétique, Bibliothèque de la Pléiade. Paris: Gallimard, 1967.
Théâtre, 2 vols., Bibliothèque de la Pléiade. Paris: Gallimard, 1959-1960.

BOOKS ABOUT PAUL CLAUDEL OR IN WHICH HIS WORK IS DISCUSSED

Andrieu, Jacques. *La Foi dans l'Œuvre de Paul Claudel.* Paris: Presses Universitaires de France, 1955.
Antoine, Gérald. *Les Cinq Grandes Odes de Claudel ou la Poésie de la Répétition,* "Lettres Modernes." Paris: M. J. Minard, 1959.
Beaumont, Ernest. *The Theme of Beatrice in the Plays of Claudel.* London: Rockliff, 1954.
Chaigne, Louis. *Vie de Paul Claudel.* Tours: Maison Mame, 1961.
Correspondance 1899-1926, Paul Claudel, André Gide. Ed. Robert Mallet. Paris: Gallimard, 1949.
Correspondance 1897-1938, Paul Claudel, Francis Jammes, Gabriel Frizeau avec des lettres de Jacques Rivière. Ed. A. Blanchet. Paris: Gallimard, 1952.
Correspondance, Jacques Rivière. Paris: Plon, 1926.
Ducard-Bourget, et al. *Claudel, Mauriac et Cie.* Paris: Editions de l'Ermite, 1951.
Gide, André. *Journal,* 3 vols. Paris: Gallimard, 1949.
Gillet, Louis. *Claudel, Péguy.* Paris: Editions du Sagittaire, 1949.
Hommage à Paul Claudel. Paris: Nouvelle Revue Française, édition spéciale, 1955.
Lesort, Paul-Henri. *Claudel par lui-même.* Paris: Editions du Seuil, 1965.
Lubac, Henri de; Bastaire, Jean. *Claudel et Péguy.* Paris: Aubier-Montaigne, 1974.
Madaule, Jacques. *Le Génie de Paul Claudel.* Paris: Desclée de Brouwer, 1933.
———. *Le Drame de Paul Claudel.* Paris: Desclée de Brouwer, 1947.
———. *Paul Claudel.* Paris: L'Arche, 1956.
Mémoires improvisés. Recueillis par Jean Amrouche. Paris: Gallimard, 1954.
Raymond, Marcel. *De Baudelaire au surréalisme.* Paris: Librairie José Corti, 1963.
Sarment, A. du. *Lettre inédite de mon parrain, Paul Claudel.* Paris: J. Gadalda, 1959.

Vachon, André. *Le Temps et l'Espace dans l'Œuvre de Paul Claudel.* Paris: Editions du Seuil, 1965.
Viscuisi, Anthony. "Order and Passion in Claudel and Dante." *French Review* XXX, March 1967.

BOOKS BY CHARLES PÉGUY

Œuvres complètes, 18 vols. Paris: Gallimard, 1953.
Œuvre poétique, Bibliothèque de la Pléiade. Paris: Gallimard, 1962.
Œuvres en prose, 2 vols. Bibliothèque de la Pléiade. Paris: Gallimard, 1959-1961.

BOOKS ABOUT PÉGUY OR IN WHICH HIS WORK IS DISCUSSED

Bonenfant, Joseph. *L'Imagination du mouvement dans l'œuvre de Péguy.* Montréal: Centre educatif et cultural, 1969.
Challaye, Félicien. *Péguy socialiste.* Brussels: Renaissance du Livre, 1954.
Christophe, Lucien. *Les grandes Heures de Charles Péguy.* Brussels: Renaissance du Livre, 1964.
─────. *Le jeune Homme Péguy.* Brussels: Renaissance du Livre, 1964.
Cimon, Paul. *Péguy et le Temps présent.* Montréal: Fides, 1964.
Delaporte, Jean. *Péguy dans son Temps et dans le nôtre.* Paris: Union générale d'éditions, 1944.
Feuillets de l'Amitié Charles Péguy. Ed. Auguste Martin.
Fraisse, Simone. *Péguy et le monde antique.* Paris: Librairie Armand Colin, 1973.
Gide, André. *Journal,* 1889-1912, vol. I. Paris: Gallimard, 1949.
─────. *Nouvelle Revue française,* XXX, I, March 1910.
Gillet, Louis. *Claudel, Péguy.* Paris: Editions du Sagittaire, 1949.
Guyon, Bernard. *L'Art de Péguy.* Cahiers de l'Amitié Charles Péguy. Paris: Labergerie, 1948.
─────. *Péguy.* Paris: Hatier, 1960.
─────. *Péguy devant Dieu.* Paris: Desclée de Brouwer, 1974.
Halévy, Daniel. *Péguy et les Cahiers de la Quinzaine.* Paris: Grasset, 1941.
Henry, André. *Bergson, Maître de Péguy.* Paris: Edition Elzévir, 1948.
Isaac, Jules. *Expériences de ma vie: Péguy.* Paris: Calmann-Lévy, 1941.
Johannet, René. *Vie et Mort de Péguy.* Paris: Flammarion, 1950.
Lettres et Entretiens. Ed. Marcel Péguy. Paris: Editions de Paris, 1954.
Lubac, Henri de; Bastaire, Jean. *Claudel et Péguy.* Paris: Aubier-Montaigne, 1974.
Mallard, Henri Victor. *La Morale de Péguy.* Paris: Editions de l'Ermite, 1952.
Maritain, Raïssa. *Les grandes Amitiés.* Paris: Desclée de Brouwer, 1949.
Poncheville, A. Mabille de. *La Jeunesse de Péguy.* Paris: Alsatia, 1943.
Quoniam, Théodore. *La Pensée de Péguy.* Paris: Bordas, 1967.
Raymond, Marcel. *De Baudelaire au Surréalisme.* Paris: Librairie José Corti, 1963.
Rolland, Romain. *Péguy,* 2 vols. Paris: Editions A. Michel, 1944.
Secrétain, Roger. *Péguy, Soldat de la verité.* Marseilles: Editions du Sagittaire, 1941.
St. Clair, M. *Galerie Privée,* "Charles Péguy." Paris: Gallimard, 1947.
Tharaud, Jean et Jérome. *Notre cher Péguy,* 2 vols. Paris: Plon, 1926.

Vadé, André. *Péguy et le monde moderne.* Quercy-Auverge: Cahiers de l'Amitié Charles Péguy, 1965.
Vigneault, Robert. *L'Univers féminin dans l'œuvre de Charles Péguy.* Montréal: Les Editions Bellarmin, 1967.
Villiers, Marjorie. *Charles Péguy — A Study in Integrity.* N.Y.: Harper and Row, 1966.

HISTORICAL AND RELIGIOUS SOURCES

Coulton, G. G. *Medieval Panorama.* Cambridge, G. Britain: University Press, 1939.
Dansette, Adrian. *Religious History of Modern France,* 2 vols. tr. John Dingle. N.Y.: Herder & Herder, 1961.
Durant, Will. *The Age of Faith.* N.Y.: Simon and Schuster, 1950.
Fowlie, Wallace, *Jacob's Night — The Religious Renaissance in France.* N.Y.: Sheed and Word, 1947.

NORTH CAROLINA STUDIES IN THE ROMANCE LANGUAGES AND LITERATURES

I.S.B.N. Prefix 0-8078-

Recent Titles

STUDIES IN HONOR OF MARIO A. PEI, edited by John Fisher and Paul A. Gaeng. 1971. (No. 114). -914-6.

DON MANUEL CAÑETE, CRONISTA LITERARIO DEL ROMANTICISMO Y DEL POS-ROMANTICISMO EN ESPAÑA, por Donald Allen Randolph. 1972. (No. 115). -915-4.

THE TEACHINGS OF SAINT LOUIS. A CRITICAL TEXT, by David O'Connell. 1972. (No. 116). -916-2.

HIGHER, HIDDEN ORDER: DESIGN AND MEANING IN THE ODES OF MALHERBE, by David Lee Rubin. 1972. (No. 117). -917-0.

JEAN DE LE MOTE "LE PARFAIT DU PAON," édition critique par Richard J. Carey. 1972. (No. 118). -918-9.

CAMUS' HELLENIC SOURCES, by Paul Archambault. 1972. (No. 119). -919-7.

FROM VULGAR LATIN TO OLD PROVENÇAL, by Frede Jensen. 1972. (No. 120). -920-0.

GOLDEN AGE DRAMA IN SPAIN: GENERAL CONSIDERATION AND UNUSUAL FEATURES, by Sturgis E. Leavitt. 1972. (No. 121). -921-9.

THE LEGEND OF THE "SIETE INFANTES DE LARA" (Refundición toledana de la crónica de 1344 versión), study and edition by Thomas A. Lathrop. 1972. (No. 122). -922-7.

STRUCTURE AND IDEOLOGY IN BOIARDO'S "ORLANDO INNAMORATO," by Andrea di Tommaso. 1972. (No. 123). -923-5.

STUDIES IN HONOR OF ALFRED G. ENGSTROM, edited by Robert T. Cargo and Emmanuel J. Mickel, Jr. 1972. (No. 124). -924-3.

A CRITICAL EDITION WITH INTRODUCTION AND NOTES OF GIL VICENTE'S "FLORESTA DE ENGANOS," by Constantine Christopher Stathatos. 1972. (No. 125). -925-1.

LI ROMANS DE WITASSE LE MOINE. Roman du treizième siècle. Édité d'après le manuscrit, fonds français 1553, de la Bibliothèque Nationale, Paris, par Denis Joseph Conlon. 1972. (No. 126). -926-X.

EL CRONISTA PEDRO DE ESCAVIAS. Una vida del Siglo XV, por Juan Bautista Avalle-Arce. 1972. (No. 127). -927-8.

AN EDITION OF THE FIRST ITALIAN TRANSLATION OF THE "CELESTINA," by Kathleen V. Kish. 1973. (No. 128). -928-6.

MOLIÈRE MOCKED. THREE CONTEMPORARY HOSTILE COMEDIES: Zélinde, Le portrait du peintre, Élomire Hypocondre, by Frederick Wright Vogler. 1973. (No. 129). -929-4.

C.-A. SAINTE-BEUVE. Chateaubriand et son groupe littéraire sous l'empire. Index alphabétique et analytique établi par Lorin A. Uffenbeck. 1973. (No. 130). -930-8.

THE ORIGINS OF THE BAROQUE CONCEPT OF "PEREGRINATIO," by Juergen Hahn. 1973. (No. 131). -931-6.

THE "AUTO SACRAMENTAL" AND THE PARABLE IN SPANISH GOLDEN AGE LITERATURE, by Donald Thaddeus Dietz. 1973. (No. 132). -932-4.

FRANCISCO DE OSUNA AND THE SPIRIT OF THE LETTER, by Laura Calvert. 1973. (No. 133). -933-2.

ITINERARIO DI AMORE: DIALETTICA DI AMORE E MORTE NELLA VITA NUOVA, by Margherita de Bonfils Templer. 1973. (No. 134). -934-0.

L'IMAGINATION POETIQUE CHEZ DU BARTAS: ELEMENTS DE SENSIBILITE BAROQUE DANS LA "CREATION DU MONDE," by Bruno Braunrot. 1973. (No. 135). -934-0.

When ordering please cite the *ISBN Prefix* plus the last four digits for each title.

Send orders to: University of North Carolina Press
Chapel Hill
North Carolina 27514
U. S. A.

NORTH CAROLINA STUDIES IN THE ROMANCE LANGUAGES AND LITERATURES

I.S.B.N. Prefix 0-8078-

Recent Titles

ARTUS DESIRE: PRIEST AND PAMPHLETEER OF THE SIXTEENTH CENTURY, by Frank S. Giese. 1973. (No. 136). -936-7.
JARDIN DE NOBLES DONZELLAS, FRAY MARTIN DE CORDOBA, by Harriet Goldberg. 1974. (No. 137). -937-5.
MYTHE ET PSYCHOLOGIE CHEZ MARIE DE FRANCE DANS "GUIGEMAR", par Antoinette Knapton. 1975. (No. 142). -942-1.
THE LYRIC POEMS OF JEHAN FROISSART: A CRITICAL EDITION, by Rob Roy McGregor, Jr. 1975. (No. 143). -943-X.
THE HISPANO-PORTUGUESE CANCIONERO OF THE HISPANIC SOCIETY OF AMERICA, by Arthur Askins. 1974. (No. 144). -944-8.
HISTORIA Y BIBLIOGRAFÍA DE LA CRÍTICA SOBRE EL "POEMA DE MÍO CID" (1750-1971), por Miguel Magnotta. 1976. (No. 145). -945-6.
LES ENCHANTEMENZ DE BRETAIGNE. AN EXTRACT FROM A THIRTEENTH CENTURY PROSE ROMANCE "LA SUITE DU MERLIN", edited by Patrick C. Smith. 1977. (No. 146). -9146-0.
THE DRAMATIC WORKS OF ÁLVARO CUBILLO DE ARAGÓN, by Shirley B. Whitaker. 1975. (No. 149). -949-9.
A CONCORDANCE TO THE "ROMAN DE LA ROSE" OF GUILLAUME DE LORRIS, by Joseph R. Danos. 1976. (No. 156). 0-88438-403-9.
POETRY AND ANTIPOETRY: A STUDY OF SELECTED ASPECTS OF MAX JACOB'S POETIC STYLE, by Annette Thau. 1976. (No. 158). -005-X.
FRANCIS PETRARCH, SIX CENTURIES LATER, by Aldo Scaglione. 1975. (No. 159).
STYLE AND STRUCTURE IN GRACIÁN'S "EL CRITICÓN", by Marcia L. Welles, 1976. (No. 160). -007-6.
MOLIERE: TRADITIONS IN CRITICISM, by Laurence Romero. 1974 (Essays, No. 1). -001-7.
CHRÉTIEN'S JEWISH GRAIL. A NEW INVESTIGATION OF THE IMAGERY AND SIGNIFICANCE OF CHRÉTIEN DE TROYES'S GRAIL EPISODE BASED UPON MEDIEVAL HEBRAIC SOURCES, by Eugene J. Weinraub. 1976. (Essays, No. 2). -002-5.
STUDIES IN TIRSO, I, by Ruth Lee Kennedy. 1974. (Essays, No. 3). -003-3.
VOLTAIRE AND THE FRENCH ACADEMY, by Karlis Racevskis. 1975. (Essays, No. 4). -004-1.
THE NOVELS OF MME RICCOBONI, by Joan Hinde Stewart. 1976. (Essays, No. 8). -008-4.
FIRE AND ICE: THE POETRY OF XAVIER VILLAURRUTIA, by Merlin H. Forster. 1976. (Essays, No. 11). -011-4.
THE THEATER OF ARTHUR ADAMOV, by John J. McCann. 1975. (Essays, No. 13). -013-0.
AN ANATOMY OF POESIS: THE PROSE POEMS OF STÉPHANE MALLARMÉ, by Ursula Franklin. 1976. (Essays, No. 16). -016-5.
LAS MEMORIAS DE GONZALO FERNÁNDEZ DE OVIEDO, Vols. I and II, by Juan Bautista Avalle-Arce. 1974. (Texts, Textual Studies, and Translations, Nos. 1 and 2). -401-2; 402-0.
GIACOMO LEOPARDI: THE WAR OF THE MICE AND THE CRABS, translated, introduced and annotated by Ernesto G. Caserta. 1976. (Texts, Textual Studies, and Translations, No. 4). -404-7.
LUIS VÉLEZ DE GUEVARA: A CRITICAL BIBLIOGRAPHY, by Mary G. Hauer. 1975. (Texts, Textual Studies, and Translations, No. 5). -405-5.
UN TRÍPTICO DEL PERÚ VIRREINAL: "EL VIRREY AMAT, EL MARQUÉS DE SOTO FLORIDO Y LA PERRICHOLI". EL "DRAMA DE DOS PALANGANAS" Y SU CIRCUNS-

---

When ordering please cite the *ISBN Prefix* plus the last four digits for each title.

Send orders to: University of North Carolina Press
                  Chapel Hill
                  North Carolina 27514
                  U. S. A.

NORTH CAROLINA STUDIES IN THE ROMANCE LANGUAGES AND LITERATURES

I.S.B.N. Prefix 0-8078-

Recent Titles

TANCIA. estudio preliminar, reedición y notas por Guillermo Lohmann Villena. 1976. (Texts, Textual Studies, and Translation, No. 15). -415-2.

LOS NARRADORES HISPANOAMERICANOS DE HOY, edited by Juan Bautista Avalle-Arce. 1973. (Symposia, No. 1). -951-0.

ESTUDIOS DE LITERATURA HISPANOAMERICANA EN HONOR A JOSÉ J. ARROM, edited by Andrew P. Debicki and Enrique Pupo-Walker. 1975. (Symposia, No. 2). -952-9.

MEDIEVAL MANUSCRIPTS AND TEXTUAL CRITICISM, edited by Christopher Kleinhenz. 1976. (Symposia, No. 4). -954-5.

SAMUEL BECKETT. THE ART OF RHETORIC. edited by Edouard Morot-Sir, Howard Harper, and Dougald McMillan III. 1976. (Symposia, No. 5). -955-3.

DELIE. CONCORDANCE, by Jerry Nash. 1976. 2 Volumes. (No. 174).

FIGURES OF REPETITION IN THE OLD PROVENÇAL LYRIC: A STUDY IN THE STYLE OF THE TROUBADOURS, by Nathaniel B. Smith. 1976. (No. 176). -9176-2.

A CRITICAL EDITION OF LE REGIME TRESUTILE ET TRESPROUFITABLE POUR CONSERVER ET GARDER LA SANTE DU CORPS HUMAIN, by Patricia Willett Cummins. 1977. (No. 177).

THE DRAMA OF SELF IN GUILLAUME APOLLINAIRE'S "ALCOOLS", by Richard Howard Stamelman. 1976. (No. 178). -9178-9.

A CRITICAL EDITION OF "LA PASSION NOSTRE SEIGNEUR" FROM MANUSCRIPT 1131 FROM THE BIBLIOTHEQUE SAINTE-GENEVIEVE, PARIS, by Edward J. Gallagher. 1976. (No. 179). -9179-7.

A QUANTITATIVE AND COMPARATIVE STUDY OF THE VOCALISM OF THE LATIN INSCRIPTIONS OF NORTH AFRICA, BRITAIN, DALMATIA, AND THE BALKANS, by Stephen William Omeltchenko. 1977. (No. 180). -9180-0.

OCTAVIEN DE SAINT-GELAIS "LE SEJOUR D'HONNEUR", edited by Joseph A. James. 1977. (No. 181). -9181-9.

A STUDY OF NOMINAL INFLECTION IN LATIN INSCRIPTIONS, by Paul A. Gaeng. 1977. (No. 182). -9182-7.

THE LIFE AND WORKS OF LUIS CARLOS LÓPEZ, by Martha S. Bazik. 1977. (No. 183). -9183-5.

"THE CORT D'AMOR". A THIRTEENTH-CENTURY ALLEGORICAL ART OF LOVE, by Lowanne E. Jones. 1977. (No. 185). -9185-1.

PHYTONYMIC DERIVATIONAL SYSTEMS IN THE ROMANCE LANGUAGES: STUDIES IN THEIR ORIGIN AND DEVELOPMENT, by Walter E. Geiger. 1978. (No. 187). -9187-8.

LANGUAGE IN GIOVANNI VERGA'S EARLY NOVELS, by Nicholas Patruno. 1977. (No. 188). -9188-6.

BLAS DE OTERO EN SU POESÍA, by Moraima de Semprún Donahue. 1977. (No. 189). -9189-4.

LA ANATOMÍA DE "EL DIABLO COJUELO": DESLINDES DEL GÉNERO ANATOMÍSTICO, por C. George Peale. 1977. (No. 191). -9191-6.

RICHARD SANS PEUR, EDITED FROM "LE ROMANT DE RICHART" AND FROM GILLES CORROZET'S "RICHART SANS PAOUR", by Denis Joseph Conlon. 1977. (No. 192). -9192-4.

MONTAIGNE AND FEMINISM, by Cecile Insdorf. 1977. (No. 194). -9194-0.

SANTIAGO F. PUGLIA, AN EARLY PHILADELPHIA PROPAGANDIST FOR SPANISH AMERICAN INDEPENDENCE, by Merle S. Simmons. 1977. (No. 195). -9195-9.

BAROQUE FICTION-MAKING. A STUDY OF GOMBERVILLE'S "POLEXANDRE", by Edward Baron Turk. 1978. (No. 196). -9196-7.

When ordering please cite the *ISBN Prefix* plus the last four digits for each title.

Send orders to: University of North Carolina Press
Chapel Hill
North Carolina 27514
U. S. A.

The Department of Romance Studies Digital Arts and Collaboration Lab at the University of North Carolina at Chapel Hill is proud to support the digitization of the North Carolina Studies in the Romance Languages and Literatures series.

www.ingramcontent.com/pod-product-compliance
Lightning Source LLC
Chambersburg PA
CBHW030237240426
43663CB00037B/1197